ALSO BY JANET G. WOITITZ

Adult Children of Alcoholics
Struggle for Intimacy
Marriage on the Rocks
Home Away from Home
The Self-Sabotage Syndrome
Healing Your Sexual Self
Lifeskills for Adult Children
Lifeskills for Adult Children Workbook

JANET G. WOITITZ, ED.D.

HEALTHY PARENTING

An Empowering Guide for
Adult Children

A FIRESIDE BOOK
Published by Simon & Schuster
New York London Toronto Sydney Tokyo Singapore

SIMON & SCHUSTER/FIRESIDE
Simon & Schuster Building
Rockefeller Center
1230 Avenue of the Americas
New York, New York 10020

Copyright © 1992 by Janet G. Woititz

Designed by Caroline Cunningham
Manufactured in the United States of America

1   3   5   7   9   10   8   6   4   2
1   3   5   7   9   10   8   6   4   2 (pbk.)

Library of Congress Cataloging-in-Publication Data

Woititz, Janet Geringer.
Healthy parenting : an empowering guide for adult children /
Janet G. Woititz.
p.   cm.
"A Fireside book."
1. Parenting—United States.   2. Adult children of dysfunctional families—
United States.   I. Title.
HQ755.8.W64 1992
649'.1—dc20   92-18058
                                                            CIP

ISBN 0-671-73948-4
ISBN 0-671-73949-2 (pbk.)

ACKNOWLEDGMENTS

Thanks to
   Betsy Geiger
   Donald Gregg
   Audrey Roberts Gregg
   Donald Hamachek
   Thomas Denham
   Jeanette Tedesco
   Zelda Weinstein

      for their expertise.

THIS BOOK IS DEDICATED TO MY CHILDREN DAVE, LISA, AND DAN, MY SON-IN-LAW DAVID, MY GRAND-CHILD REBECCA, MY STEPCHILDREN SANDRA AND PAUL, MY FOSTER CHILD BETH, AND MY ADOPTED CHILDREN JONATHAN AND MIRIAM. THEY HAVE TAUGHT ME THE SPECIAL JOYS OF PARENTING AND HAVE MADE SURE THAT I EXPERIENCED ALL THE STRUGGLES, ANXIETIES, AND FAILURES THAT SEPARATE THEORY FROM PRACTICE.

AND TO BERNIE, FOR HIS INFINITE AND LOVING PATIENCE AND SUPPORT.

Contents

Preface   11

ONE
Healthy and Unhealthy Parenting Patterns:
An Overview   19

TWO
Defining the Roles   34

THREE
Overcoming Negative Messages   44

FOUR
Loving versus Shaming   56

FIVE
Understanding Boundaries   65

SIX
TOLERATING FEELINGS   80

SEVEN
THE PARENT AS TEACHER AND GUIDE   87

EIGHT
SETTING REASONABLE LIMITS   97

NINE
STAGES OF CHILD DEVELOPMENT   113

TEN
LIVING WITH LOVE   130

ELEVEN
LEARNING HOW TO PLAN   139

TWELVE
SPECIAL CONSIDERATIONS   153

THIRTEEN
TAKING CARE OF YOURSELF   177

FOURTEEN
LOOKING BACK AND LOOKING FORWARD   182

CLOSING   186

HEALTHY PARENTING

PREFACE

PARENTING IS ONE of the most difficult jobs anyone has to face, and one for which most of us are poorly equipped. The idea of having a baby is wonderful and terrifying at the same time. But who among us contemplating becoming a parent for the first time also considers that the baby will, in short order, become a two-year-old, an eight-year-old, and, G-d help us, an adolescent?

The decision to become a parent is largely a selfish one. One decides to have a baby for a number of self-fulfilling reasons. People have babies because babies are love objects, or because they want their seed perpetuated, or because their biological clock is ticking. Some want to offer a new life what they never had and thereby reduce their own sense of deprivation. Others find themselves parenting other people's children when they take a new partner whose children were born prior to the relationship and are therefore part of the package.

The reasons to have children have primarily to do with what we want out of life and not with the new life we create and his or her demands. There is nothing wrong with this. It actually makes very good sense, because more often than not as we make this decision the new life does not exist yet except in the world of fantasy.

So, unless you have been through the process before, the idea that this wonderful bundle will change your whole life—that things will never be the same again—is a hard one to conceptualize.

If you come from a healthy family, you will have a model of child rearing that you can use as you begin this process. You may also get some useful direction from your family. If you come from a troubled family, chances are that what you learned is what you *don't* want for yourself and your family. But knowing what you don't want does *not* tell you what you *do* want or how to get it.

The goals of parenting are simply expressed. They are to raise physically and emotionally healthy individuals who will develop self-reliance and purpose in their lives. We begin by recognizing that children have rights and that it is the job of parents to be sure those rights can be exercised:

A Child's Bill of Rights

I have a right to live rather than exist.

I have a right to personhood rather than being an object of possession.

I have a right to equality with every other human being regardless of age.

I have a right to be respected with regard to my worth.

I have a right to be uniquely myself with my own identity.

I have a right to speak my thoughts and feelings, and to be heard.

I have a right to ask "Why?" and to receive answers.

I have a right to receive discipline without being hollered at, discounted, or put down.

I have a right to be encouraged to grow to maturity at my own pace.

I have a right to be free from physical harm at the hands of resentful people.

I have a right to be loved for being me.

*I have a right, with valid guidance, to think for myself, and to make
my own decisions.*

I have a right to be responsible for myself.

*I have a right to feel joy, happiness, sorrow, bereavement, anger,
and pain.*

I have a right to be a winner.

*I have a right to care and be cared for, to nurture and to be nur-
tured, to give and receive.*

I have a right to form my own convictions, beliefs, and standards.

I have a right to know and experience personal freedom.

*I have a right to my own body, mind, and soul, and to use them in
a sharing experience.*

*I have the right to recognize and accept the rights of others regarding
their Bill of Rights.*

—Fred

This book is designed to let you know the particular pitfalls
you will face in respecting that Child's Bill of Rights if you grew
up in a troubled family.

What is a troubled family? It is a family that is adult-centered
and in which the needs of children do not come first. Troubled
families often result when parents are chronically ill, either mentally or physically, or are addicted to alcohol or other mind-
altering substances. But they can also result when families experience other types of loss or upheaval, including divorce, death,
economic reverses, frequent relocation, or other causes. We'll
talk about this in more depth in the next chapter.

If you come from a dysfunctional family, this book will help
sort out for you the areas of your greatest confusion and provide
ways to assist you in making more appropriate decisions. It will
teach you ways to keep the past from interfering with the present
in unhealthy ways.

Some families are dysfunctional for a time, then things work
out. If you come from one of these families, you are likely to be
more in the "mid-range." You are probably less confused than
the child of a perpetually dysfunctional family. You already have

a level of awareness of what was wrong and what was right about your childhood. So, your need will be one of achieving additional clarity on the matter. This additional awareness will probably show you how to change the patterns you need to change. You don't have to be living in an extreme situation or come from a profoundly traumatic background to benefit from the principles described in this book. As with anything else, there will be some things that make sense to you and other things that don't, but you will find there are choices available to you.

You might think you come from a dysfunctional family if you didn't get along with your parents when you were a teenager or if you got yelled at every time you walked in the door. But if this is the full extent of the friction in your household, you probably did not come from a dysfunctional family. In a typical family children become angry at their parents in order to collect the leverage they need to comfortably leave home. This dynamic usually begins in the teenage years as children need to try things "their way" and parents struggle to keep some control in their own household. This situation is not a dysfunctional one unless things get totally out of control. It is a healthy one. Ironically, adolescents who are *not* at odds with their parents are more likely to live in a dysfunctional situation than kids who are.

So if you were able to be centered in your life, if you are able to make the decisions you need to make and are comfortable seeking advice when you can't figure it out on your own, if you believe you are essentially a good and capable person and you are lovable and capable of loving, if you believe you can share and be shared with, if you believe you can communicate and be communicated with, if you believe life is something worth experiencing and have values you believe are worth passing on even if you are angry at your parents or are panicked at the responsibility of becoming one yourself, chances are that your family system was a relatively healthy one.

If this describes you, the comparisons you will find in this book should prove useful indicators. Even if you identify with some of the unhealthy patterns, the ability to make those changes will be stronger in you than it will in the child of a dysfunctional family, who will have to work harder but can also achieve the same results.

In summary, if you are someone who never feels ineffective as a parent—regardless of whether or not your parent was alcoholic or absent in other, less dramatic ways—this is a book you should read.

Whatever your history may be, if you're panicked at the thought that you're going to screw it all up, if you fear you're so badly damaged you do not have the right to bring another person into the world, this is a book you should read.

When people are expecting children, some degree of anxiety is normal—will we have a healthy baby? Can we be effective parents? These questions and others like them are part of the universal condition. Anyone who is blasé about having children and the responsibilities they are taking on is of greater concern to me than those who are somewhat anxious about it, because it is appropriate to be anxious.

If the anxiety is crippling, that is something else. If you feel a sense of terror that you may be inadequate to this job, you may need to seek the help of a professional, and through that help either ease some of the anxiety or decide that having children is a responsibility you don't have to take on. Sometimes people panic because they feel they are too badly damaged themselves. And sometimes people panic because, in effect, they are about to reproduce to serve the needs and desires of others rather than themselves. Although there are many things we may do to please others, giving birth to a child should not be one of them.

A look at this book will help to put these fears and others into perspective. It will also help you if you think your anxiety level about becoming a parent is a normal one, but you do come from a troubled family and you want to be sure. If you do feel a little overanxious about damaging your kids and come from one of these families, the book will help you to do a little work beforehand and somewhat ease your anxiety.

The reality is that we all bring a legacy with us from our

childhood. And we all remember things we didn't like about the way our parents raised us, patterns we fear we'll repeat ourselves as we raise our children. Some of these fears are simple and superficial. For example, our parental legacy may cause us to retch when we see somebody dunk a doughnut. But other aspects of our legacy may have greater consequences, such as feeling rejecting toward a child who fails a math test. When we see these things in ourselves, it is apparent to us that we are just like our mother or just like our father. We dislike these things in ourselves, yet we feel powerless to change them. By exploring the deeper implications of these attitudes, and in addressing those implications, we are empowered to make changes in our parenting style.

So, in effect, although people from dysfunctional families may identify most with what's said in these pages, it is probably also true there will be something here virtually everybody can identify with. This fact is not a judgment on any of us as parents. It just provides an opportunity to make the responsibility of parenting more rewarding for everyone.

Whatever your reason for coming to this book, as in every other aspect of your life you are probably fearful you are not capable of doing it "right." Don't be concerned with being inept. We are all inept. Some just hide it better than others.

All children behave in ways that create problems for their parents. You, like all other parents, have to deal with these problems. Parenting is a big job if done conscientiously. When you become a parent, you can be sure there will be times of extreme joy and times of unbelievable frustration. There will be moments of great pride and of great embarrassment.

There will also be times when the love you feel will fill you to bursting and times when you can't understand what made you decide to become a parent in the first place. It is all part of the package. It is true for all of us.

This range of feeling will be especially difficult for you to manage if you grew up in a dysfunctional family, because as you feel it, you will constantly worry if you are reacting appropriately.

Your lack of a healthy model will lead to your developing certain myths as to what a good parent should be like. For instance, one myth is you should be just like the parents on television. Therefore, if you are a good parent you'll never get angry at your children. You'll never feel you are at your wits' end.

Or, if you are a good parent you will be able to handle each situation as it arises intelligently and with relative calm. All problems will have nice, tidy solutions. This is nothing more than wishful thinking. The only people who have all the right answers are those who have not been humbled by the experience of having children of their own.

If you grew up in a dysfunctional family, you are no doubt frightened and confused at the very idea of being a parent. It just seems so overwhelming. It is so important to do it right, and yet you feel so hopelessly insecure. After all, what background do you have for providing a healthy environment for your family? You know from your own experience what you *don't* want to happen again. But that experience in and of itself does not prepare you to make your own family different. That will come with awareness and hard work.

Learning how to be an effective parent is a part of your growth process. Just as your personal growth comes with awareness and hard work, so does parenting. Both come with the initial acceptance that without help, life is unmanageable. This is true of anyone who wants to do a good job, regardless of their history. You cannot do that good job without support, just as you cannot do your personal recovery without support.

As you begin to read this book, you may find you are becoming flooded with the memories of your own abuse and deprivation as a child. You may become aware of ways that you are repeating earlier patterns. You will probably feel sad and angry.

These are understandable responses. If this happens, and there is a very good chance it will, because you have only your own experience to draw on and much of that is troublesome, I recommend you read the book through—feel whatever you need to feel for yourself—and then take whatever steps you need to take care of these feelings. You may want to join a support group, or get professional help. Or, you might want to take a little time to try and distance yourself from the material in order to put it into perspective. Or, it may be enough simply to talk to others who grew up in families like yours.

The object is to learn to separate out your feelings and be able to focus on the needs of the child. This is very difficult to do when feelings surface and overwhelm. It is not possible to attend to the needs of the self and the child's needs at the same time. You may end up looking at your family history in a way you haven't done before. You may feel a variety of emotions stemming from rage to profound grief. This is not surprising if you have not gone through this process before. You need to process your reactions first, to desensitize yourself first.

When you've done that, go back and read the book again with your children or prospective children in mind. This time, focus on how to offer *them* what *they* need. Focus on how you can create a different environment for your children.

Separating all of this out will be difficult, so don't be discouraged if you have trouble with it. That's what this book is all about. Just stay with it until you can do it. It's difficult, but it can be done. The bottom line is that your children cannot provide for you what your parents did not. They cannot make up for your losses. But you *can* provide these things for your children. Your awareness of how bad it felt when your parent forgot your birthday or didn't come to the school play or embarrassed you in public will help you be sure that you offer a different life for *your* children. You can then feel joy in and with their joy, and in the knowledge that you are breaking the cycle.

There is no reason to be discouraged. The information you need and the help you require are both available. This book will be a major step in your journey toward healthy parenting.

O N E

HEALTHY AND UNHEALTHY
PARENTING PATTERNS:
AN OVERVIEW

FOR THE LAST twenty years I have worked with individuals who grew up in troubled families. My job has been to help make them aware of how their past experience has impacted on their present functioning and to help them develop new patterns of reaction and behavior.

Nowhere does the result of growing up in a dysfunctional system manifest itself more blatantly than in the area of relationships. For the child of a troubled family, the struggle to develop loving and responsive relationships is overwhelming.

These individuals' concerns are endless:

Am I capable of loving?
Am I worthy of being loved?
Am I too demanding?
Am I not demanding enough?
Are my expectations realistic?
Can I fulfill someone else's expectations?
Can I care for someone and not lose myself?

These questions come up in all intimate relationships. But for the child of a troubled family, the pain of not being able to reconcile such concerns is very great. The anxiety that builds up is enormous. The self-doubt leads many to wonder if it is worth it to try to become involved in meaningful relationships at all.

The intimate relationship between parent and child brings additional concerns:

Is it fair for someone as damaged as me to bring a helpless
    child into the world?
Will I end up being just like my mother/father?
Do I have the right to have a baby just because I want to?
What if he/she inherits my alcoholism?

The questioning is exhausting. The reassurances are understood intellectually, but the emotional torment goes on. The decision to have a child is certainly not one to be made lightly, but neither is it one that can be made only after all the doubts are resolved.

The questions I am asked most often are: What is normal? Is this healthy? Did I do the right things? Is there something wrong with my child? Do other people have these problems?

Without an understanding of what is normal every aspect of parenting provokes great anxiety. The questions that must be addressed to resolve this anxiety are simple.

Do I want to have a child?

Am I willing to work hard (with assistance) to provide a nurturing and healthy environment for this child?

John and Marie are fairly typical of couples who, having grown up in dysfunctional families, are confused about how to be good parents. They came to see me because they were concerned about their thirteen-year-old son, Eddie. Eddie was becoming very unmanageable at home. His school grades were erratic, and his coach said he had an "attitude problem." This was not like him, they said, and they needed help to figure out what to do.

John said, "I wouldn't dare have spoken to my father the way Eddie talks to me. My dad was a violent drunk and if I so much as looked out of line I'd get beaten 'til I bled. I've tried so hard to give my son a better life than I had. But he's never satisfied."

Marie had tears in her eyes. "My mother had multiple sclerosis and needed constant care. I spent my childhood taking care of her and helping around the house. I ask so little of Eddie and he resents anything I ask. What am I doing wrong?"

The reason Eddie is so challenging for them is that they can't look back on their own childhoods and remember what they were like at that age. The reality is that they are not doing anything wrong. Unlike Eddie, John and Marie's teenage years were spent caretaking and being invisible. So a reflective look back into their own childhoods isn't useful. They won't find examples of what being a normal teenager is like there.

The reality is that most teenagers have "attitude problems." Authority figures are to be tolerated at best, but certainly not to be given credit for having any intelligence. It is part of the struggle of growing up. Neither John nor Marie got to be a typical thirteen-year-old. They grew up in dysfunctional families and missed out on their childhoods. They have no idea what a normal childhood is all about.

Although Eddie's behavior is not unusual for a child of his age, it doesn't make it any more acceptable or easy to live with.

But there is a certain comfort in the knowledge that at least he is not crazy and his parents haven't damaged him. The lack of a frame of reference makes parenting much harder.

I know a mother named Cynthia who went out and bought a whole wardrobe of beautiful little dresses for her five-year-old daughter, Nan. When Nan refused to wear the dresses and kicked and screamed and told her mother she hated them, Cynthia became terrified that something was wrong with her daughter. In effect, all that was going on was that Nan wanted to dress in jeans like all the other five-year-olds but Cynthia had a fanciful notion of what little girls should look like.

Cynthia came to me for advice, very disturbed about the incident. She wasn't disturbed about the possibility that buying the dresses was a mistake. What concerned her was that her child didn't want to wear the clothes she had purchased for her.

When we talked, it turned out that Cynthia had gotten her notions of what a family was supposed to be like from watching television. Cynthia had been a "latchkey" kid. Both her parents had worked, and she had grown up in an isolated country setting, far away from other children, and caring for herself in the afternoons. Cynthia had attended a parochial school that required uniforms, and when she came home she longingly admired the frilly little dresses the girls wore on TV, which she watched incessantly.

Cynthia didn't want Nan to have to endure the same severe wardrobe she'd had to endure in her own childhood, or the same severe childhood, for that matter. Nonetheless, she didn't think to include her child's wishes in the design of her own wardrobe. Instead, Cynthia wanted her daughter to play out her own fantasies of what an ideal childhood should be. Nan wanted to be her own person and resisted. When she did, Cynthia became very concerned about her. But the truth is that her kid was just fine.

Usually what is going on in one family is fairly similar to what is going on in other families with children of the same age.

Nevertheless, for those who come from dysfunctional family systems, the anxiety that results from the combination of not knowing what those typical behaviors are and of wanting so desperately to be a good parent is very great.

It is my belief that with very few exceptions, no one deliberately creates a harmful environment for children. Nonetheless, it happens. However, lack of knowledge of how to create a good environment and lack of malevolent intent do not absolve one of responsibility.

If I did not see you and I hit you with my car, you are still hurt. Because I didn't mean it does not make your bones any less broken. This is also true for you as a parent. Without taking deliberate steps to behave differently than your own parents, the patterns of your childhood will repeat themselves regardless of whether or not you want them to. To break this cycle, you need to become aware of the unhealthy patterns you are perpetuating and learn how to change them.

Bear in mind that all your questions deserve to be answered and you need to continue to hunt out the answers until they are. The specific answers will vary from family to family but the principles for finding those answers are the same for every family. This book is based on ten of those principles. While they are not all-inclusive, they will serve to help you isolate your own unhealthy patterns and replace them with healthy alternatives.

You did not have parents who were positive role models so you will have to ask and ask and ask. You also didn't get to go through the developmental stages that kids go through in the usual way. You may have had to take care of others rather than be taken care of at the age other kids had very little responsibility. You may have kept a low profile because of fear of violence at stages where other kids were oppositional and testing authority. As a result, you cannot use your own history as a frame of reference.

What follows is a partial list of what healthy is and what unhealthy is. If you identify any aspects of the unhealthy pattern as your life experience, then pay particular attention to the healthy counterpart. You may not even have been aware that the pattern you knew was unhealthy. No need to beat yourself up over it. After all, it is all you knew.

1. a) In a healthy family the job of the parents is to take care of the children.
b) In an unhealthy family the job of the children is to take care of the parents.

2. a) In a healthy family the messages are clear and understood. If they are not, they can be questioned.
b) In an unhealthy family there are double messages, leading to confusion and guessing.

3. a) In a healthy family the child is always loved even if the child's behavior is unacceptable.
b) In an unhealthy family the child is shamed and the person is confused with the behavior.

4. a) In a healthy family personal boundaries are respected.
b) In an unhealthy family personal boundaries are unclear and often violated.

5. a) In a healthy family all feelings are tolerated.
b) In an unhealthy family feelings are often violated and are therefore repressed.

6. a) In a healthy family the parent is a teacher and guide.
b) In an unhealthy family the children bring themselves up the best they can.

7. a) In a healthy family there are reasonable limits and structure.
b) In an unhealthy family there is chaos or extreme rigidity.

8. a) In a healthy family demands made on children are age- and developmentally appropriate.
b) In an unhealthy family the child is asked to demonstrate pseudomaturity or is infantilized.

9. a) In a healthy family children are affirmed regularly and automatically.
b) In an unhealthy family children are made to feel unworthy and unlovable.

10. a) In a healthy family there is organization and planning as well as the ability to respond to a crisis.
b) In an unhealthy family the members respond from one crisis to the next, and when crises don't exist, create them.

If your life experience was b and you want the life experience of your children to be a, then there is a great deal to learn. Desire for change does not automatically make change happen, but the "how" of doing it can be learned. The patterns can be changed.

In a healthy family much attention is paid to the growth and development of the children. Their physical and emotional needs are consistently met and the child feels safe, valued, and loved.

The child knows with 100% certainty that someone will be there to take care of him. He knows his thoughts and feelings will be listened to and considered important. Experiencing consistent nurturing and love are his birthright. All these things are his, automatically and unconditionally. He owes nothing in return. He is special because he exists. He does not have to earn these things. He can trust that his family will be there for him and that this trust will not be violated. Home is a refuge from the world and a place where energy is spent making the world safe as well.

In a dysfunctional family the needs of the children are not of major concern. Their needs are not the main focus. The family is not child-centered. The physical needs may or may not be attended to, but the emotional needs are met inconsistently, if at all, and rarely, if ever, in terms of what the child wants and needs. The focus in a dysfunctional family is to make children compliant and to reduce parental stress. The child as a person with her own needs and desires is lost in the process. Families that are dysfunctional in this sense result largely from parents who are chronically ill, either mentally or physically, or are addicted to alcohol or other mind-altering substances.

Other stressful systems that, without careful management, have strong potential for trouble include those where the family is experiencing loss either through death, divorce, or an absentee parent; blended families; those where there is only one parent, remarriage, or adoption; and those where there are economic reverses resulting in a change of lifestyle, or where there is much relocation. The potential for trouble exists because each of these situations creates a dynamic in which the needs of the parents can override the needs of the children, temporarily or more permanently. In each of these situations, the child-centered structure of the healthy family can be put at risk. This can happen without warning and without intent. New circumstances can overwhelm and roles can become confused.

Careful management means becoming aware of developing patterns and changing them as a result of this new awareness. Some causes and effects are predictable and need to be addressed. For example, Holocaust survivors tend to be distrustful. With an understanding of where his parents' distrust comes from, the survivors' child may be able to moderate his responses to this trait. Without such an understanding, chances are that this child will perceive the world in much the same way his parents do. Even though the child's response will be a normal one—to imitate his parents—the consequences to that child's perception of himself will be different and may seriously impact on his self-esteem.

Lorraine spent a lot of time when she was growing up trying to prove to her mother that her brother was not an only child. No matter what Lorraine did, it wasn't good enough. And as a result, any achievement of hers just became a new bottom line. As a result, Lorraine became a towering model of accomplishment. There was always something that could be improved upon and meeting her mother's approval became Lorraine's life work.

Lorraine now has children of her own, and Lorraine's daughter Marcia is wonderful simply because she is wonderful. Yet one day during her freshman year at college, Marcia called Lorraine on the phone.

"Mom, I can't get out of bed," Marcia told her mother.

Lorraine asked Marcia what the problem was.

She replied, "Well, I'm taking a full course load, I'm managing the college radio station, I'm directing the hot line, I've taken a job at night parking cars three miles away, and I have to walk there because I melted my car engine."

Oh my G-d, thought Lorraine. She wants to be just like me.

So Lorraine went up to see Marcia and they talked about what was possible for her to do and what was not possible for her to do, and how to prioritize her time. Lorraine also made sure Marcia knew she didn't have to prove anything to her mother.

If Lorraine had not been aware of her own mother's influence on her and the power of that influence, she would not have been aware of her own influence on Marcia and the power it had. Had Lorraine not intervened, Marcia would have either flunked out or dropped out. There was no other option available to her. As a result, Marcia's self-image would have been damaged because she would have concluded she was not as good as her mother, after all.

But since Lorraine and Marcia were able to work on this process together, Marcia was able to put her life in order and finish her education in a manner that made sense.

Without intervention like Lorraine's with Marcia (possible only because Lorraine had become aware of the influence her own family's parenting had had upon her), these highly charged parenting styles can evolve to the point where they resemble the management styles in workplaces whose employers are from dysfunctional systems. In a sense, the workplace becomes a home away from home. The same themes tend to play out in the workplace that play out in the home situation, and the same behaviors one exhibits as a parent one also exhibits as an employer. Without intervention, the responses of employees are not very dissimilar from the responses of such employers' children, so without intervention the same styles perpetuate themselves. It is important for you to know about this connection because you need to be able to make the distinction between home and work.

For example, it's not at all unusual to see a man who barks orders all day in the workplace to repeat the same behavior when he enters his home. This behavior may be acceptable in the work environment, but not in the home. Or, such a man may behave in exactly the opposite manner at home. But neither style is functional.

The nature of the stressors in the family does not necessarily determine the parenting style. There is no predictability. The styles develop as a survival mechanism for the parent. They are the response to the parent's own background. However, the response on the part of the child is somewhat more predictable.

As you read this chart, see if you can identify the patterns of your own childhood. Did your parents fall into one or more of these categories? If they did, be aware of your own responses to that environment.

PARENTING STYLE	CHILD'S RESPONSE
The Overcritical Parent: *This parent examines everything with a judgmental eye. Nothing is good enough. A flaw will always be found. Praise is withheld. Constant criticism is the norm.*	*The child struggles to please in order to gain approval and/or love. The more they are withheld, the hungrier the child gets for them. He is always hopeful that this time will be different, this time he will be good enough. The child sees himself as flawed and inadequate. As an adult he will never feel satisfied with what he does or with what others do.*

The Overdemanding Parent:

This parent places unrealistic demands on herself. She takes on more than is humanly possible and sees no alternative. This parent also has unrealistic expectations of her children in terms of what she expects them to accomplish around the house, in school, and after school.

Even if the child believes that the demands are unfair, she will try to comply. It is a way of proving self-worth. Compliance with this parenting style means giving up childhood. There is no playtime. The time is used up fulfilling the parent's desires. As an adult this child will either become workaholic or drop out.

The Promiser:

This parent gets the children to comply by offering rewards. If you do this, then I will get you that or take you there. The parent has every intention of doing as he says but somehow is never quite able to pull it off. Since there was positive intent the child is expected to take this into account and not be angry or upset.

The lure works and even after many disappointments the child will still believe that this time will be different. If the child gets angry or disappointed, he is made to feel guilty because (1) the request should have been followed simply because he is a family member, and (2) next time it will be different. In adulthood this child is untrusting and asks nothing for himself.

The Absentee or Ineffective Parent:

This parent either works or is out of the house for long periods of time or can't get it together when she is home, either out of drunkenness, physical problems, or inadequacy.

The response of the child is to take over the household and take care of the household responsibilities. The child becomes the parent in the household to both siblings and parents and loses out on being a child. As an adult, this child will become a caretaker and may refuse to have children of his own.

The Dictatorial or Indifferent Parent:

This parent is nonparticipatory. He leaves the child to take care of herself or dictates to the child without room for discussion.

The child feels unwanted and unrespected: if she were cared about, she would at least be involved with the process of what to do and/or how to do it. As an adult, this child fears abandonment and is slow to relate.

The Rescuing Parent:

This style is to become enmeshed with the child and to do everything for the child without allowing for emotional separation or the possibility of error. The child is infantilized.

The child feels dependent and inadequate. Separation causes panic. This response is encouraged even though the parent complains about how fearful the child is. As an adult this person either pushes others away or loses himself in a relationship.

There is, of course, overlap in the parenting styles and in the children's typical reactions. The purpose of this list is to show some of the general responses to dysfunctional lifestyles and is, to an extent, oversimplified. It is by no means a thorough discussion but is intended to indicate probable cause and effect. Intervening variables can modify, exaggerate, or complicate responses. You don't have to identify with all of these parenting styles or typical responses, nor does it mean that because you experienced one of these styles you'll suffer from them all.

Some of these styles are only dysfunctional when they are carried to an extreme. For example, the typical "Jewish mother" style of parenting can contain overcritical aspects. But while a parent who uses this style may, as the old joke goes, ask the child who wears one of two ties the parent gave him what was so wrong with the other one, this does not imply that the child is worthless. It implies that although the child may be phenomenally successful and a wonderful human being, he should continue to seek his mother's approval. Such messages often also contain an educational aspect. Perhaps the green tie would have gone better with the khaki-colored suit than the blue one does.

On the other hand, the parent whose style is dysfunctionally overcritical transmits only the message of worthlessness and criticism, while the love is withheld: "Don't you know better than to wear that tie with that suit?" The overcritical parent may not take the time or have the inclination to offer suggestions or alternatives the way the functionally critical parent does. And even if he or she does, the child may feel so put down it becomes difficult to absorb such suggestions if and when they are given.

We may all have a little bit of all of the aforementioned styles within us. There is nothing wrong with that. It is when there is no balance in our parenting style that this style leads to unbalanced responses in our children. A parenting style *has* to be eclectic in order to be balanced.

The concept that is undeniable, however, is that dysfunctional parenting styles lead to emotional struggles for children. These children, when grown, will lead their lives in reaction to their past without knowing how to offer a wholesome environment to their own children.

The idea is to break these patterns and provide a more healthy and balanced environment. Without the awareness of how you responded as a child, you will tend to (1) repeat the pattern because the style is familiar and internalized, or (2) be the opposite so as not to repeat the pattern.

Everyone is concerned about being a good parent to their children. But if you had no role models you respect, as a parent you tend to have to make things up. As a result, it's not unusual to end up being over- or underinvolved, overcritical or not discerning enough, too controlling or not controlling enough in your parenting style.

The notion of balance simply is not available to you because you have no role model for it. You don't know how to be balanced because you don't possess the necessary data for weighing one set of options against another in order to come up with a measured and informed decision. So you concern yourself with how a situation will look on the outside instead of concerning yourself with the actual building blocks that will add up to the sound structure that transmits the wonderful-looking family image. This lack of data, this lack of building blocks, results in new dysfunctional and troubled families. It can also simply result in a lot of unnecessary anxiety.

If your parents were hypervigilant because of their own fears, you may tend to be super-watchful as well. If you found such vigilance suffocating, you may be hypovigilant with your own children and as a result not be watchful where you need to be.

When Arthur and his small children moved into their new house, even though it was a very nice house in a very nice neighborhood he began to feel very overprotective of them. One evening he was sitting in the den with two of his children waiting for the babysitter to arrive when he happened to notice a white car pass by the front of the house.

About ten minutes later he thought he saw the same car drive past the other way. About the fifth time the white car drove by the house Arthur began to become very concerned about his children's safety, particularly since he would be out for the evening. He decided that if the car drove by one more time he would call the police.

It did and he did.

The policeman rang Arthur's doorbell almost instantly.

"I'm so glad you came so promptly," Arthur said.

"Aren't you curious why I got here so fast?" the policeman asked. "I was the one in the white car, patrolling your neighborhood. I was practically in your driveway when you called."

Arthur had to laugh. He realized he had been watching the street so closely because as a child he was watched so closely. His children were perfectly safe.

The point is, if you come from a dysfunctional family, it can be hard to know when to be vigilant and when to ease up. If you have concerns like this, you may want to consult other parents. You may be fearful about your child walking to school by himself. And you may wonder if other parents share this concern.

They may or may not. The best way to discover the answer could be to ask them.

The ideal is to learn when to be cautious and when to allow the child to explore. You wouldn't want to teach your child to ride a bicycle on a busy street. That would be dangerous. If your child suggests this, and she will, caution is called for. But in response to your child's desire, rather than only giving an emphatic no or launching into a discussion about bicycle safety, you might want to find a place where there is no risk your child will bump into something or be bumped into, and in such an environment, encourage your child to explore her new skill unhindered by concerns for her safety.

In parenting, neither extreme response to a situation is effective. Effective parenting styles emerge from knowing how the past impacts on the present, knowing how to keep what works, and knowing when to discard what doesn't. The next step is to develop the tools that will enable you to offer a safe, nurturing environment where healthy growth and maturity are fostered.

T W O

DEFINING THE ROLES

a) In a healthy family the job of the parents is to take care of the children.

b) In an unhealthy family the job of the children is to take care of the parents.

I REMEMBER AN eight-year-old who woke up in the middle of the night and found her mother on the floor, overdosed on drugs. The girl called the paramedics and rode to the hospital with her mother. The child's quick action saved the mother's life.

The little girl was referred to me because she was having nightmares. When I asked her to tell me about those nightmares, she said they were all the same. "I wake up in a panic with one thought in my head. What if I hadn't woken up and found her?"

This is not a child's nightmare. A child's nightmare would be about the fear of losing her mother. But this little girl was afraid that if she were not there for her mother, her mother would die.

The roles had reversed. She had become the mother to her mother. Her childhood had been taken away from her. If childhood means a time where one is relatively carefree, when one can play without worry, where one can be dependent, then this eight-year-old was clearly not a child.

The outcome of the accident was that the girl's mother went into treatment for her addiction and stopped using drugs. She entered a recovery program and, little by little, tried to be a mother. Meanwhile, the little girl stayed in therapy and addressed her trauma and her loss.

I saw her recently. She is an adult now and is unmarried and childless.

"I am so happy being responsible only for me," she said. "I may never marry or have children. There are those who say I'll miss out and maybe I will, but for now this feels wonderful."

Not all parentified children make the same decision as adults.

Bruce has chosen to become a parent and struggles against his past. He called me one day in turmoil. He had just received a call from his son's school. Jamie had had an accident in gym class, and although it didn't appear that any bones were broken, he was in quite a bit of pain. Could Bruce please pick him up and have him checked out?

Bruce said, "I told them I would come, but I'm so enraged that I thought I should call you first. How can he do that to me! Jamie knows I'm in the middle of an important deal. I can't just walk out of here in the middle of the day. To hell with it. He'll just have to wait."

"Aren't you forgetting something?" I asked. "You're the parent. It is not Jamie's job to take care of you and sit around in pain until it's convenient for you to come and get him. It's your job to take care of him even if his timing is inconvenient for you."

Bruce was taken aback. "I can't believe you said that. I thought you of all people would understand. Okay, wait a minute . . . I get it. It's my mother again. That's what you're trying to tell me. During my growing up years, my job was always to take care of her feelings. It was up to me to make sure that nothing disturbed her. So if I was in my kid's place right now, I would deny my pain rather than let my school call my mother. *Her* happiness was my main concern and if anything displeased her, *my* life wasn't worth living. The guilt I felt if I had to ask for anything was overwhelming. I've only just become aware that I have a right to have feelings, too. But on the other hand I don't want to be like her. It's so darn hard to separate all of these feelings out!"

The feelings surfacing for Bruce are the ones he repressed as a child, so they are the feelings of a needy kid. The child in Bruce wishes Jamie could put his father's needs first, because Bruce's mother never did that for him. At the same time, part of Bruce also assumes Jamie will behave as Bruce did when he was a child and denying his own needs. This is because in childhood, that was the pattern Bruce knew. The wounds left over from Bruce's childhood run very deep.

If the pattern is to be changed, as difficult as it is, Bruce has to put his own feelings aside and concern himself with Jamie and being there for Jamie.

If you consider only your needs, or even if you consider your needs before those of your children, you will end up perpetuating your own childhood pattern. Your child will fall victim to your own childhood. Your child needs to know that he is important enough to you for you to drop everything and be there for him.

Bruce was able to put his feelings aside and go to the school. Jamie was so relieved and happy to see him that he spontaneously threw his arms around his father and wept. His father did the same. As a result, both of them got their needs met and a valuable lesson was learned. When Bruce showed Jamie how much he loved him, Jamie responded in a loving way. The son gave his father love not because it was his "job," but because that was what was in his heart.

Beverly Sills, the noted soprano, was being interviewed about her involvement with the March of Dimes. She shared with the reporter the fact that her daughter had a birth defect and as a result had a profound hearing loss. The reporter commented on how tragic it was that the child was unable to hear her mother's magnificent voice.

"Do you ever ask yourself, 'Why me?' " the reporter enquired.

"Never," said Beverly. "But I do ask, 'Why her?' "

In a dysfunctional family, the child's needs are not considered. It is more the reverse. In these families it is the child's job to keep the parent happy or at the very least appeased. It is up to the child to be there for the parent, not the reverse.

The child adapts to the situation. The joys of childhood are kept secret because if they are expressed they will be spoiled. The angers of childhood are kept silent because they will not be supported and they will cause the child more problems. The fears of childhood are pushed aside because they will be mocked and minimized. The self is squashed.

The child, if the parent is chronically ill or alcoholic, may prepare food for and clean up after the parent. The child, if the parent is depressed, may ease and calm the parent's fears.

Another way that the roles get confused is when the child is made to fill in for a neglectful or absent spouse.

How many times have I heard after a divorce, "Now, you're the man of the house." Or, about a drunken mother, "You're a better cook than she ever was!"

When you grew up there was role distortion. It was not unusual for you to be a parent to your parent. You knew it wasn't good for you to be a parent to your parent. You resented it but there was no way around it. In a way which you didn't understand, it made you feel important. This role wasn't good for you, and it's not good for your children, either.

If your children end up replacing, ever so subtly, an absent or neglectful spouse, it will distort the parent-child relationships and get in the way of the children relating to their own peers appropriately. Taking care of you will feel like their primary job, before others. Even if it made you feel important, it was not the appropriate role for a child.

You may argue and say, "But she loves it when she comes

along as my date," or, "He feels important when I put him at the head of the table when we have company." That does *not* mean it's okay. That gives children an inflated sense of their importance and they will feel superior to their peers. Next children will begin to find their peers "so immature" that they will end up isolated from them. If your child enjoys playing that role in your life, and children usually do, it will make it that much more difficult for him or her to relate to kids his or her own age. Why go to the movies with a clumsy sixteen-year-old when you can go with your dad or your mom? Why go and eat french fries at the diner when you can have an elegant French dinner?

It sets the child up to have more difficulty separating from you and connecting with their own age group. Children have fantasies about their parents anyway, and it is important that they don't become real.

A child who ends up trying to substitute for an adult in a parent's life is the same child who hurries home after school to make sure everything is in order instead of playing baseball or going to a friend's house. As a result, this child may go through his adolescence later, at a much more inconvenient time. This child will feel guilty about abandoning the parent when it is time to go to college, and the parent will play into this guilt: "I don't know how I'll get along without you, but don't worry about it."

This child will feel obligated to keep checking in with the parent. Whereas a college kid from a functional family may say to another, "My parents are laying a guilt trip on me because I don't want to go home during spring break, but I'm going to do what I want to do," the parentified child will be too overwhelmed with guilt to make the same decision. As a result, this young person will continue to not develop socially, or, going to the other extreme, will act out socially. Eventually he will develop relationships in which he plays the role of the caretaker. He will be drawn toward the "helpless" type. And resent it.

Many parents living in abusive situations will bring their children into their bed in the hopes that the presence of the children will reduce the chance of violence when the offending spouse returns home.

Some will bring a child into the bed as a way of avoiding sexual contact with their partner.

A therapist I know reported, "I had a couple seeing me last year where this was an issue. When the husband came in late, the nine-year-old and five-year-old daughters would be in bed with their mom."

The husband got the message: "I don't want you in bed when you're stinking drunk and I certainly don't want to have sex with you."

The mother convinced herself she was comforting her daughters, who were upset when Daddy was out late at night. She had difficulty seeing how she used the girls as a buffer from her husband and as comfort for her own grief and loneliness in the marriage.

Others will let a child sleep with them because the child wants to be close to them and the parents don't want to bother with the trips back and forth, back and forth.

The child belongs in his or her own bed. With the exception of the first year of life, the separation of parent and child helps in the individuation process which is essential for the child's emotional well-being.

Bear in mind that bringing your children into your bed is putting your needs ahead of theirs. It decreases your anxiety, and although the children will look forward to it, it is not in their best interest.

They need their privacy and you need yours. Teaching appropriate boundaries is part of the role of a parent.

Not replacing an absent spouse doesn't mean children should not take on additional responsibilities to fill the gap. The child should not fill the missing parent's social role, but the child may have to take on some more of the household chores.

It is usually a good idea to plan out with the children who will do what and when. It may be that everyone takes a turn fixing a meal or mowing the lawn. These chores get shared because family members need to share responsibilities in the house and for no other reason. The children don't take on new roles, just new chores.

The idea is, we are a family and we all have to pitch in more whether we like the idea or not. I can understand you not liking the idea, but that doesn't mean you don't have to do it. It just means it's okay for you to feel that way. Who among us would do chores if we didn't have to? Demonstrating that you are aware of and can be clear about describing their appropriate role will help the children feel secure.

In a dysfunctional family, such distinctions are not made, let alone clearly. As a result, roles get distorted and it is difficult to determine who is the parent and who is the child.

In a dysfunctional family, it is not unusual for a five-year-old to be taking care of younger siblings, nor for an eight-year-old to prepare all the meals for the family.

Children in these families run home from school fearful that Mom will have choked in her own vomit, or have set fire to the house. Children lie sleepless waiting for their fathers to come home, praying that he will arrive in one piece.

Children like these are never free of worry or anxiety. They are unable to be spontaneous and fun-loving. Taking care of their parents is their job.

If this is what your home was like and you are now a parent, the experience of providing a childhood for your children will be a new one for you. It will be up to you to create an environment for them that is free of anxiety and worry. It is up to you to encourage them to be carefree and to be spontaneous. It is up to you to make them feel safe.

When you think to yourself "Why me?" or when you get unbelievably frustrated that your five-year-old can't tie his own shoe or another glass of milk got spilled, bear in mind that what your kids are doing is being kids and that your losing control is not being responsive to them. It is serving your own need. You can make them feel bad that they're not smart enough for you or careful enough for you, but that won't make them smarter or more careful. It will just make them feel bad about themselves and sorry they disappointed you. Their job is not to keep you free from disappointment or frustration. Their job is to be kids. And if they please you or make you proud along the way, that is a fringe benefit. But it is not their job.

The need to have control can go to extremes. A patient named Ben told me that when his mother caught him playing with matches as a young child she took his finger and put it in the hot flame. Until he revealed this experience to me, this father of four had not had any idea how abusive it was. But Ben's mother had thought she could control her son with pain, that she could extinguish his inconvenient and childlike behavior in this way.

Fear is an effective means of controlling behavior. But it is not an effective means of helping a child develop his own sense of responsibility and appropriateness. Things like keeping matches out of a child's reach and telling children of the risks matches pose are a far better response to this particular problem.

You will probably have a more compliant child if you use the more drastic means. But compliance for its own sake is not a goal of parenting, because it serves the needs of the parents, not the needs of the child. Yes, you'll be in control, but the person that your child is and will become will be damaged in the process. And when someone is controlled in childhood by fear of pain or bodily harm, that same person in adulthood will not know other ways to discipline her own children. As a result, it is very likely that as a parent this person will use some form of physical response in order to get a child to conform. Once again the abusive pattern will be perpetuated.

Take the time to teach your child to tie his shoelaces. Or, buy Velcro. Give your child a sponge to help wipe up the milk, or give her a cup that won't spill. It may be that the impatience you are feeling is a throwback to the way you were treated, and you are repeating the pattern. So when those feelings surface, count to ten and remind yourself that you are the grown-up.

Although this discussion is heavily weighted to demonstrate

your role as a parent in meeting the needs of your children, it is also important to point out that your needs are important as well and do not *always* take second place.

Jean had a three o'clock appointment and was in a rush to get there on time. Just then, her three-year-old son informed her that he wanted Jean to read him a story *now*.

You are not being an abusive parent if you tell the child that he or she will have to wait until later, that you are in a hurry and can't do it right now. The fact that the child may object and nudge does not change anything. If you are *always* in a hurry and can't ever accommodate your child, then that is something to look at. But dropping everything because the child has a want is not good for anyone, either.

As our children get older, all of us go through the experience of lending a teenager our car against our better judgment, only to have the child have an accident. (This has the same predictability as the child spilling some juice the first time she drinks out of a glass.) After we determine the child is not hurt, it is our turn.

I recall how the daughter of a friend of mine parked her mother's new car at the curb only to have a snow plow scratch it. The girl called her mother, hysterical.

The mother's response was quite simple and to the point.

"Oh no, my dear," she said. "You don't get to be hysterical over this one. It is my turn."

The teenager was careless with the car and did not garage it as she had been told after a large snowstorm was predicted. Kids are kids. Your job is to allow them to be kids, and then get it out of your system for yourself. You can't have it both ways. In other words, you can't allow them to be kids and then reprimand them for it.

The bottom line is, I am the parent and you are the child. As the parent, I am responsible for your well-being. It is up to me to provide for your basic needs of food, clothing, and shelter. It is also up to me to be responsive to your emotional needs as you mature, and to teach you and assist you in dealing with the outside world and in learning to become a responsible member of the family. It is up to me to make your home a safe and welcoming place. My love for you is without qualification. Your job as a child is to grow and develop and behave as a member of the family, with age-appropriate limits and responsibilities.

THREE

Overcoming

Negative Messages

a) *In a healthy family the messages are clear and understood. If they are not, they can be questioned.*

b) *In an unhealthy family there are double messages, leading to confusion and guessing.*

SANDI RECALLS, "My mother was a great promiser. She would promise to come to the school play or watch me play ball and then she'd get drunk and not show. She even missed my graduation. If I got upset or angry when she let me down and told her so, she'd yell at me and I'd feel terrible that I had caused her trouble.

"I swore I'd never be like her. I stay away from alcohol and I do my best to be there for my daughter. I can't always because I am going to school and working two jobs and it simply isn't possible. What I just realized as I was talking is that when my daughter complains about my missing a game, instead of being sympathetic with her feelings I get defensive and make her feel bad that she is adding to my burdens. I'm going to change that. How easy it is to fall into that trap."

It is so confusing. "I'll be there . . . next time." I'll be home in time for your birthday party. I'll take you to the ball game on Saturday. Let's go shopping together.

If you had a parent who was a promiser, at the time these promises were made to you they felt sincere. You believed them. You needed to. And even when it didn't happen and a new promise was made, you believed that, too. Eventually over many years you learned the truth. It just wasn't going to happen—not ever. For some of you it would happen every once in a while, which only made it harder for you the rest of the time.

A broken promise is one kind of mixed message. What Luke heard from his father is another kind.

Luke relates, "My father was deeply distrustful of anyone who was college educated. The only honest day's work was with your hands. Yet he made it very clear that I had to get good grades so that I could go to college and have a better life than he did. I was very confused. I wanted his trust, but I also wanted to fulfill his expectations. As a result, wherever I am I always feel like I don't really belong."

If you had a parent who gave you mixed messages, this had to impact on you in a variety of ways. Firstly, you learned not to trust. If you trusted, you would be disappointed, and there is a limit to how much disappointment one kid can handle. As a result, when you grew up, people who offered you things or opportunities were viewed with suspicion. You feared either they would disappoint you, or that if they came through they must have an ulterior motive. No one could be trusted. It didn't matter who they were.

Secondly, you became inflexible. If you had one set of plans, that plan was set in concrete, and other options, regardless of their value, you invariably rejected. If someone offered another idea it would flip you right back into your childhood tape. You would understand this new idea as a broken promise and as a result you would feel violated. Any value the new idea held was lost.

Thirdly, you became very sensitive to lying. You became an expert liar yourself and you became particularly tuned in to the slightest nuance of an implication that you were not being dealt with honestly. It was one of the ways you learned to survive.

This has to impact on your parenting. You will naturally want to warn your children that nobody is to be trusted. Even if you don't voice your opinion, your children will learn it from you by your example.

The reality is that some people are to be trusted and others are not.

You do need to teach your children not to trust certain people in certain situations. Don't accept a gift from a stranger. Don't get in a car with a stranger. Don't even talk to strangers unless you are with an adult and the adult says it's okay.

However, you can teach your children to trust you. You can demonstrate that your word is good. You can show them that when you make a promise, you will keep it.

The children will need to learn that in the world there are those they can rely on and others they cannot. As a result, sometimes life will work out as they hope and other times it won't. Disappointment is as much a part of life as joy. The major difference between experiencing disappointment in a functional family and in a dysfunctional one is that in the latter you were disappointed by those who were closest to you. You were let down by those you automatically go to for comfort. If you are a conscientious parent, then you will be a source of strength for your children and when the world lets them down they can run to you for comfort with certainty that you will offer it.

When their little hearts are broken because they weren't picked for the team, or because they weren't invited to the birthday party, or because Patti doesn't want to be their friend anymore or because their favorite toy was broken, it is so important for them to know you will be there to help ease their wounds so they can face the next day. If you had an overcritical or hyper-vigilant parent, keep in mind that this is not the time to tell them you warned them if or you told them they shouldn't . . . It is the time to just be there with a hug, an open heart, and a willingness to listen. Somehow, that makes everything so much better.

Sooner or later, and probably sooner, your child will need to receive exactly this reassurance from you at a moment when your attention is diverted elsewhere; at a moment when, because of your history, giving the reassurance is inconvenient. As a result you may be tempted to send your child that most common of mixed messages: "I love you, go away."

Although the child is told she is loved and although the child believes this to be true, if the parent is too often otherwise occupied there is a sense that she is underfoot. This happens regardless of whether the parent who sends this message is the father who tells his kid how proud he is of her and then goes back in the den to work after dinner or the mother who chooses to brag about the child's accomplishments on the phone instead of spending any time with her.

The result of this mixed message is that when the child becomes an adult, she will be very attracted to people who reject her. And to feel as though those people who are there for her consistently—those who always call when they say they will call and those who are always there when they say they will be—hold no interest. Such an adult may find her own children's needs of her time and energy to be suffocating. As a result, the pattern may be perpetuated as she tells them through her words that she loves them while at the same time her actions indicate a desire for distance.

The clear version of this mixed message is: "I love you, come here." Love is behavior. The child needs to feel and experience the love, not just interpret the words.

Instead of going straight to his study, that same father could spend five or ten minutes with his kid. Or, if the father has no option but to work, he could invite the child to come in and quietly do her homework while he met his own obligations. The mother singing the child's praises on the phone could tell the child directly to her face how proud she felt as well.

Your tendency to be rigid about decisions or plans that have been made will definitely require adjustment on your part if you want your children to have certain feelings and to learn certain skills. In order for children to feel like a part of the family and in order for them to learn how to cooperate and how to carry on a conversation, it is necessary that they be allowed input in making family plans and decisions. That doesn't mean the children are given the power to make such decisions, it just means their thoughts are taken into account as those decisions are made.

Keep in mind that children will probably not participate "right" right off the bat. First they will have to learn how and then they will get civilized through practice. Until they do, their response to someone else's idea will probably be a putdown: "Eeeeeeew—icky!" Or, "Who'd want to see a dumb movie like that?" Or, "Spareribs are disgusting."

When this happens, the idea is not to leave the room enraged, but rather, to ask them if they have another idea.

You can even teach very young children to brainstorm. The idea is to have each person put in an idea. You make a rule that nobody can put anybody else's idea down. Then each person gives his or her idea in turn. Keep going until all ideas are out on the table. Then the good ideas are discussed and a decision is made. You can still be the one to make the decision, but it is important for you to allow others to have a voice. Something like this might be the result: "Okay, I'll tell you what. We'll go out for hamburgers tonight because that's the closest place, but next time we'll go for Chinese."

All kids lie. But because of your history with mixed messages, when your kids lie—and they will—it will make you nuts. Young children often have imaginary playmates, and they will not only tell you about them but accuse them of being the one who really spilled the milk. The cartoon *Calvin & Hobbes* offers a superb example of an imaginary playmate. To Calvin, his toy tiger is just as real as he can be. So let your child have his imaginary playmate and recognize that he has a rich fantasy life. It is not something to worry about at this stage.

As they get older, children's reasons for lying shift. "I knew if you knew the truth you would be angry, so I figured if I lied there was a chance you wouldn't find out and I'd get away with it, and if you did find out you'd be angry but I would have bought a little time." This is how the logic usually goes.

Logic like this is clear to children, but can be enraging to a parent—especially one to whom lying was a way of life in his or her own childhood.

The only response a parent can give is (1) "The consequences will be greater for you if you lie," and (2) "If you lie to me then I will lose respect for you and I will not be able to trust anything you tell me. One day the time will come when it will be very important to you that I believe what you are telling me. But if you have lied to me in the past, chances are I'll be suspicious even if you are telling the truth."

With my kids that line of reasoning would go right to their heartstrings and would be very effective until the next time they thought it made even more sense to see if they could pull one over on me than it did to be truthful.

A main point to remember is that children build their sense of self and their self-esteem from the clear, precise messages they get from the significant adults in their lives—most especially their parents.

Reflect back on your own childhood. What did your parents say when they complimented you? What did they say when they criticized you? What was their main advice to you?

If you grew up in a troubled family, compliments were few and far between. You also felt constantly criticized. Many of you cannot be specific as to what the compliments and criticisms were. You just kind of recognized them by the expression on your parents' faces.

A sense of self is built by using the specific input that you are offered by your parents. "Do your best" may be the advice that a parent gives to a child, but it is confusing advice. How do I know what my best is? "Act like a lady." What does a lady act like? "You can be anything you want to be." How do I do it?

"Do your best" or "Act like a lady" have absolutely no meaning. When we say things like this we all think we know what we're talking about until someone *asks* us what we're talking about. So if your kid is nervous about taking a history test, instead of just telling him, "Do your best," validate his feelings. You could do this by saying, "I used to feel that way sometimes when I was your age. Sometimes I would get so anxious before a test I'd be afraid I wouldn't be able to see the paper. But somehow I got through it and you'll get through it too, and as long as you've studied, that's good enough for me."

This kind of information helps give children a sense of self. The more general type doesn't. Besides, if kids don't get specific input of this kind they tend to make it up for themselves instead. For instance, they learn to know whether or not their father is angry by the way he walks into the house. This is why when I have asked students of mine to recall the compliments or criticisms they got from their parents when they were children, it is not unusual for them to say they don't remember having received any. When we trace back, we find their lack of memory has nothing to do with whether or not they were able to remember. It has to do with the fact that there weren't any.

There was no concrete input from their parents for them to build on about their behavior or about anything else. These children grew up in a data vacuum. As a result, it was hard for them to develop a sense of self, because they had nothing to build it on. I often hear, "I want to be accepted for who I am." But when I say, "Fine, I'm happy to do that, but who are you?" the person who expressed the need doesn't know.

The reason they don't know is because they did not get specific instruction from their parents that they could use in developing a self. This is where the lack of a data base for parenting begins. And it is also the result of that lack of data base when it is perpetuated into the next generation.

Luz's parents would always tell her how pretty she was, often at family gatherings or at other times when they felt proud of her. They didn't give her more specific information on why they were proud, but merely complimented her appearance.

When it was time to leave home and go to college, Luz felt directionless. She went to school because she was "supposed to," but soon dropped out to pursue a career in modeling, right before it was time to pick a major. Luz's career was not satisfying to her. Although she was somewhat successful at it, her finances were very insecure and the competitive atmosphere was very uncomfortable and sometimes even hurtful to this girl with a very sensitive personality. When people whose opinion Luz valued got specific with her and suggested she begin to think about other options because she wasn't happy, she would get angry and turn against them.

As time went on, Luz's small success dwindled. She became even more unhappy and more unfocused. But she kept at it until finally work stopped coming in altogether. Finally, at the age of twenty-five, she returned home and reenrolled in the local college.

Luz feels frustrated and embarrassed that she is still directionless. She is still asking people she respects what she should do with her life, but now she is listening to their answers.

There is nothing wrong with becoming a model if you want to be a model and being a model is fulfilling for you. But Luz devoted herself to being pretty because that was all she had. If you were told you were pretty and nothing else when you were a child and you know it pleases your parents to think of you as pretty, then as an adult you devote yourself to being pretty.

If you raise kids with generalities, chances are that the process of making life decisions will be confusing to them. Chances are, it will take them longer to figure out the rest of life. They will have to learn to do it themselves.

So give your kids as much detail and input as possible about everything you can think of. This helps to give them a blueprint for life that they can either accept or reject in favor of some

other, equally detailed blueprint. But they need to have the basic
data for life to come up with their own version.

Don't worry that you might give them too much information.
If you provide too much information, your children will stop
paying attention to you. When that happens, just slow up.

I also often hear, "My parents never complimented me directly. I think they were afraid I'd get a swelled head, but I often
ended up hearing the good things they'd say about me from other
people. I wish they'd told me. If they thought well of me, why
didn't they tell me? It would have made such a difference."

This is another example of a situation in which your needs
as a child were not primary. Your need to be supported and
encouraged by your parents was ignored in favor of your parents'
need to brag. If I tell you that you are wonderful, it belongs to
you. If I tell my neighbor that you are wonderful and my neighbor
is impressed, it belongs to me. I am the one being complimented.

Be sure you tell your children what they do well and what
was good about it. Some examples of specific compliments are:

"That shirt looks terrific with those pants."
"What a delicious salad. The onion makes all the difference."
"You are a fast runner."
"You sure know how to tell a joke."
"You have such a nice, quiet style."
"What a great idea. Let's test it out."

This will not be that easy to do because you did not have
the experience of being complimented yourself. So complimenting may not come naturally to you. But remember that lack
of input is perceived as negative input. I suggest you conscientiously make an effort to compliment or be supportive of your
children—without a "but"—and to make this effort every day.
It doesn't have to be big. "What a lovely smile you have."
"Thanks for picking up those newspapers." "I enjoy sitting with
you."

One of the things that makes this hard is the double message many of you remember receiving as children. "You can't do any-thing right. I need you." That set you up to try and try, because you knew you were needed but you were never able to satisfy. No matter what you did it wasn't good enough. No matter how hard you tried you couldn't cut it. As a result, this was an image that became a part of how you see yourself. What this means is that you will automatically see the flaws not only in everything you do but in everything your children do. You will always know a better way.

You are going to have to bite your lip. "That's a very sweet thank-you note you wrote to your Aunt Sarah." You don't have to tell your daughter she started too low on the page. It simply doesn't matter. If you point it out "for her own good" or so "she'll know better next time," your child will feel like a failure and any joy she felt in writing the note will be lost.

This will be very hard for you, but if you can remember how demoralized you were by the constant criticism you received as a child, maybe that will help. Anything you can do to enhance a child's self-image is good parenting.

Next time you can suggest she start higher on the page if you want. But the key thing is that the child is learning a social skill.

I'm not suggesting you never correct. Aunt Sarah will be upset if you leave off the *h* in her name. But be sure when you do so that your correction is useful and not degrading, and that the criticism is not just the result of your own perfectionism.

Remember too that when you were told you couldn't do anything right, it went to the heart of you as a human being. It said, in effect, that you were stupid. Not that you made a mistake.

There is a world of difference. If you are stupid, that is who you are and you are stuck with it. If you just *do* something stupid, then you can learn a better way.

So when your children behave like "airheads," and they will, no doubt about that one, be very careful not to call them names. You may have to point out the mistake, but that is different.

The kind of thing I mean when I say "airhead" is the kind of thing kids do all the time: forget their lunch, forget their permission slip, leave the project home on the day it was due after they spent six weeks on it, and on and on.

This is the kind of stuff that drives a parent crazy. But the kid didn't do it on purpose. Her head was simply elsewhere. The dilemma for the parent is how to handle this. It isn't as if you didn't remind her or leave it in front of her face so she wouldn't miss it. Keep in mind that she doesn't do it just to aggravate you, as difficult as that is to believe. She just does it because that's what kids do.

A good rule of thumb to apply here is, "If I let the child feel the full consequence of his action, will I be punished? And, is the full consequence equal to the crime?"

I don't believe when the child does something because his attention is elsewhere that his attention will improve because lack of it created problems for him. That may turn out to be the case if it happens often enough, but a short attention span is typical of kids.

So I say to myself, I will not be hungry if he forgot his lunch. And chances are, I would let that be the child's problem.

If the permission slip was for a trip that would enable me to have a couple of free hours, I might make the effort to deliver it.

And if the truth be known, I think a lot of parenting involves saving a child from himself. Children's tendency to self-destruct is beyond belief. So if I had the time, I would probably have mercy and bring the project to school so the kid wouldn't be marked down after putting in all that effort.

How you handle matters like this is up to you, but you can't take any of it personally. It simply doesn't pay to get bent out of shape over behavior that is part of growing up.

You are in charge of the self-esteem of your children. It is your input that they will carry with them throughout their lives. Be sure you are clear in what you say, and that whenever possible, you frame things in a positive way. There is no doubt that doing so can be quite an exercise.

A friend of mine named Bruce Caruth, one of the most

supportive people I have ever known, always finds a way to get his point across without ever making a negative comment.

I was a guest at his home one weekend and his wife made some muffins that would have had to improve in order to be terrible. His wife and I agreed they really didn't work out. I said to her, "I can hardly wait to hear what Bruce says."

Not too much later Bruce came down to breakfast, sat down, took a bite out of the muffin, replaced it in his napkin, and said, "Boy, are the dogs going to love these muffins!"

Make a game out of it for yourself. It will help to change the habit. Remember, the goal is to break the cycle. And the closer its pitfalls come to your consciousness, the easier breaking that cycle will be for you.

LOVING VERSUS SHAMING

a) In a healthy family the child is always loved even if the child's behavior is unacceptable.

b) In an unhealthy family the child is shamed and the person is confused with the behavior.

I MET A man in Canada who said to me, "I keep reading about how important hugs are to mental health. In my family no one hugged. They didn't even touch, and I hate being touched. My kids climb all over me and it makes my skin crawl. Even so, I force myself to hug them and be close. I'm glad that I can give them what they need even if it doesn't feel good to me."

One of the ways parents demonstrate love for children is by holding them and making them feel warm and secure. It's one of the very first things we do for children when they are born. We are encouraged to hold them. Studies with baby monkeys have shown us that when they receive no physical nurturance, the newborns may die. Holding a child fills a very basic need, and deprivation causes psychological damage.

Even though he was denied touch in his own childhood, the man from Canada has made a very deep commitment to loving his own children. He is aware of his old childhood pattern, and he has made the effort to change that pattern as he parents his own children.

But this man has also experienced shame. Even though intellectually he knows it isn't true, on a very deep level this father still believes that had he been worthy of nurturance he would have received it. Not touching or hugging your children may cause them to feel shame.

Others who were deprived in this way during childhood will have the opposite reaction from the one my Canadian friend had. He had to force himself to touch his children. In contrast, others will find they will not be able to take their hands off their own kids.

Both types of parents need to learn balance and how to separate out their needs for love and touching from those of their kids.

Ironically enough, if someone says to you "Can I have a hug?" and you hug them, it feels different than if someone says to you "Can I give you a hug?" and hugs you. To the observer, the two acts may look identical. But to the participant, the results are entirely different. To one who doesn't recognize this difference it can be very confusing.

If you are hugged and it serves your need, it helps to fill you up emotionally. But if you are asked to hug, and hugging doesn't serve your need, you may end up feeling depleted. If you are a child, you will end up feeling shamed as well.

I knew a little girl with an alcoholic mother. When this mother had been drinking she used to sit in the eight-year-old's lap and insist that the child rock her. Today that eight-year-old child is a woman who is just beginning not to be repulsed by someone who cares about her and wants to put her arms around her. She has no children of her own.

Children can be shamed in many other ways. Children who

are shamed in any way end up believing they are not worthy of love. They come to believe they are unlovable.

If you tell your children they are a problem in your life; if you tell your children you can't stand the sight of them; if you tell your children you wish they'd never been born, that "You are bad," they will *not* look at you and realize you have lost control and don't mean it—they are children, not adults.

On the contrary. They will believe every word of what you say and take every word to heart. If they were lovable, you wouldn't feel that way and you wouldn't say those things. As a result, they will come to know in their hearts that they are unworthy of love. Once this happens, they will come to hunger for your love, but they will have great difficulty making close friendships or forming close social relationships. They will grow up believing it is their fault they are not loved at home, that there is something awful within them that has caused you to withhold your love. They will believe that anyone who likes them has been fooled by them. They will keep others at a distance. Closeness will not be available to them. They will have short-term intense relationships, because that will reduce the pain of their shame if only for the moment.

It also means they will have trouble leaving home when the time comes. They will still crave your love and be fearful of others. The reason they will still crave your love is that they never received the love they needed from you, so they stay, hoping that part of themselves will eventually be satisfied.

This need is very basic to us as human beings and is one that must be met through our parents. Many people who are in therapy are there essentially to get this unmet need met. In successful therapy, the therapist comes to fulfill the role of the parent for the client. This process is called *transference*. When it occurs, the client can enter the process of getting those early needs met. And when he leaves therapy, it is because he has grown beyond the intense need to be nurtured by the parent who wasn't there for him.

If you offer your children unconditional love while they are young, they will feel confident they are worthy of love. And when the time comes, they will be able to leave home with more inner security. This means they will be able to establish significant new relationships and at the same time continue to connect with you.

Unconditional love means the following: I love you with no strings attached, regardless of how you behave. This doesn't mean I always accept your behavior, but it does mean I always accept you as a person.

Because of your history you may not be able to offer unconditional love to your children automatically. This is not something to beat yourself up over. What it is, is something to be very mindful of. *Always* separate the child from her behavior. This ability is not unlike what you learn to do if you survive with an alcoholic. You learn to separate the person from the disease.

I cannot caution you enough about the repercussions of name-calling or ridiculing a child's behavior. The results can be devastating. Losing control on your part for whatever reason is not an acceptable excuse for shaming a child in this way. Think about your own childhood and what it did to you when you were put down and made to feel worthless. If you can keep this in mind, it may help to short-circuit your mouth.

Children are also shamed when they are criticized and humiliated in public. They are shamed when their parents devalue their things or do not show up for the ball game or teacher-parent conferences. They are shamed when they do not live up to their parents' expectations of them, if they are told they are not good-looking enough or thin enough or smart enough, or if they do not make the choices their parents want them to make.

I'm reminded of a little boy whose father picked his nose in public. He was mortified and tried to pretend they were not together. He judged himself for being embarrassed by his father, but knew he was embarrassed by him. The child couldn't tell his father, because he was afraid he would be angry at him. As a result, he stuffed his true feelings and tried to avoid being seen with his father.

All shaming attitudes leave children feeling emotionally debilitated and that their true self must be hidden at all costs. The result is that they don't share their feelings and they avoid interaction with other children. This is done partly to preserve a piece of themselves, and partly to keep the world from knowing who they really are and therefore being disgusted by them.

Shaming children strikes at their core, so shove your need to be truthful to them down your throat until you know that what you are saying and how you are saying it serves a useful purpose.

Parents shame because they are out of control. If you grew up in an abusive home you may have been humiliated when the neighbors saw your father staggering home drunk or when your parents fought so loudly they could be heard down the block. Even now, just recalling those circumstances may fill you with shame. Be careful you do not lose control in the same way and behave in ways that will embarrass your own children. If you do, they too will carry those memories into adulthood and cringe at the thought that these family secrets will be exposed.

This is a very tough assignment, especially if you were shamed as a child and as a result shame is what you know. But there is a payoff for both you and your children if you break this cycle.

Sara relates, "I remember driving my mother and two of my kids to the mall. The kids were acting up in the back seat and wouldn't listen to reason. My mother turned around and said to them, 'If you loved me you wouldn't behave that way, because it upsets me when you do that.' Classic shaming behavior. And I said, 'That worked on me, Ma, but it won't work on them. But this will.' And I pulled over to the side of the road and said to the kids, 'Are you going to behave or are you going to walk home?' That worked. What my mother said worked on me because she was my mother and I responded to her as my mother. But because I was aware of what it did to me when I was a kid, I very conscientiously did not do that with my own children."

Chances are that with your history, as a child you too were controlled by the loss of, or fear of the withdrawal of, love. This means that if you were not compliant or if your parent was not in a loving mood, you felt the emotional abandonment. This was a very desperate way for you to feel, and you would have done just about anything to avoid experiencing that feeling. You hungered for love, and probably still do.

This is an unconscionable way to treat a child. Unconditional love is a child's birthright. A child has the right to feel with 100% certainty that she is loved.

That does not mean she is always liked and that does not mean she does not sometimes drive you up a wall. It does not mean the child will not get you furious. It just means that 'love' and 'like' should not be confused.

Somehow in troubled homes there is a lot of confusion about what it means to be angry. There is often the belief that:

"If I love you I can't be angry with you."
"If you love me you can't be angry with me."
"If we love each other we have no angry feelings toward each other."

This is not so. Frankly, it often works in the opposite way. Only the folks who really matter to us are worth the energy it takes to be angry.

So, as a parent you need to clearly separate these things out. Instead of unconsciously sending these messages:

"I will not love you if you do not do as I say."
"And I will not accept you if you do not do as I say."

Separate things out so you send these instead:

"I love you, but I do not always love the things you do."
"I accept you unconditionally, but will not accept unacceptable behavior."

Yes, it is true that withholding love is an effective way to manipulate a child to conform. But you will not get the desired result in the long run. You will bring up an insecure child and one who changes his behavior not because he has learned a better way, but because he fears abandonment.

As an adult, this person will constantly seek the approval of others and become what we call a people pleaser. A people pleaser doesn't really have an inner sense of self-worth. A people pleaser will also relate to others the same way the parent does, making honest relationships impossible. When you shame a child, you undermine the child's self-worth.

If your child is gay or lesbian, issues that come up around sexuality and sexual identity can also be shame-based:

"My brother Tom is gay and he's a marginal member of the family. He was a sissy when we were growing up, so I wasn't surprised. I don't have any problem with it as long as he doesn't come near my boys. One of them reminds me of my brother so I go riding with him and make him play sports. One in a family is enough."

When George expresses his homophobia he has no idea of the emotional impact this will have on his son. But the truth is, the profound shame his attitude induces can inflict lifelong scars.

If you have a child who is gay or lesbian or who you suspect is gay or lesbian, it does *not* mean you have done anything wrong and it does *not* mean there is anything wrong with your child.

Your children want your approval. If your child believes he is homosexual and that you do not approve or will love him less or not at all if you know, the shame he will experience will have a profound impact on his life. As a result, he will:

1. Deny his sexuality to himself and others;
2. Be ashamed of his true feelings and be ashamed of himself for having these feelings;

3. Not be truthful about his responses to things so as to be like everybody else;
4. Behave as if he were straight and have a secret life;
5. Blame all his problems on his sexuality and become homophobic.

All of these responses will lead to confusion and deep psychic pain for the child. It is therefore very important for you to overcome whatever difficulties, if any, that you have with this knowledge.

If you are troubled about the sexuality of your children, do not hesitate to talk to a professional or to join a support group of parents with gay children.

It is critical to the emotional well-being of your child that you are loving and supportive and nonjudgmental regardless of how difficult it is for you.

None of us ever hear that we are loved too much. None of us ever tire of hearing that we are special. We all take pleasure in hearing caring words, and our children take pleasure in that as well. Hearing someone say "You know that I love you" does not satisfy us as adults when caring actions are lacking, and it does not satisfy our children, either.

A friend of mind tells of a day when she was washing crystals on a very ornate and delicate chandelier. Betsy was a nervous wreck, and to make matters worse her five-year-old daughter kept coming into the room and Betsy kept shooing her out.

Finally, the little girl just stuck her head in and said, "Mommy, would you just tell me one thing? Do you still love me?"

"Oh my G-d! I'm so sorry. I'm just afraid that I'm going to drop something, and I haven't been fair to you. Yes, I love you dearly. Please just give me a little more time and then we can be together."

The reassurance was all the child needed. After this conversation, she was able to wait for her mother to be finished. Fortunately, the child was able to ask the question, so she didn't begin to doubt her own lovableness.

Keep this in mind. It's so easy to blame ourselves even when there is no reason. Our children are this way, too. Therefore, it's important to reassure our children of our love even when we know they already know it.

F   I   V   E

UNDERSTANDING
BOUNDARIES

a) In a healthy family personal boundaries are respected.

*b) In an unhealthy family personal boundaries are unclear
and often violated.*

"From when I was about eight years old until I was maybe eleven or twelve," Jeff says, "my mother was having an affair. My parents were separated and my father lived two hundred and fifty miles away. This man was a friend of my mother's family and also a doctor and he was frequently at our house. I was told never to mention the fact that he was there so often to my dad or their marriage would split up. I never saw my mother and this guy engaged in any overt physical intimacy, but he and his family always seemed to conveniently be where we were on vacations and there always seemed to be a reason for him to be at our house. I was aware that something was wrong but I didn't know exactly what or why, and I felt a split in the allegiance among Mom and Dad and me and I didn't understand why I felt that way.

"All my life my mother told me she was the only one who I should trust, yet by then I knew I had watched her betray my father constantly.

"When my parents got back together after three years of separation—I was twelve at that point—Mom started accusing Dad of sleeping with other women. She would find some seemingly incriminating evidence and would rant and rave about it in front of me until he got home and then would loudly confront him. It wasn't fair to me. I shouldn't have had to listen to this. It makes me sick to think back on all of this. No wonder I have trust and boundary issues now.

"I am trying hard to learn a healthy balance between interest on the one hand and intrusion on the other hand. I am so insecure with my own kids as to where the boundaries are. Am I being too controlling? Am I being too permissive? I don't know when to demand that they go to bed, do their homework. I don't even know when to put my foot down about their taking a bath. When am I being a good parent and enforcing boundaries? When am I going too far and interfering and controlling too much? I spend a lot of time in therapy working on this, because I am determined to be different from my mother. I'd never want anyone to interfere and control any kid the way she controlled me."

Personal boundaries involve an individual's right to his own:

1. Thoughts
2. Feelings
3. Possessions
4. Space
5. Body

Jeff's mother did not respect his right to his own thoughts, feelings, or space. She did not allow him to have his own opinions about her actions, or to have his own feelings about her relationships, or to have a safe and nurturing space to call his home.

If you grew up in a dysfunctional family, what I have listed above may be new information for you. You may not have a sense of what appropriate boundaries are for yourself and for others. Learning what appropriate boundaries are and respecting them when you do will be a big task. It is important to know where other people end and you begin. It is important to learn how to separate this out.

1. CHILDREN HAVE A RIGHT TO THEIR OWN THOUGHTS.

If you grew up with anarchy, order will be important to you as an adult. You will want to know very clearly who is in charge. Who the parent is and who the child is will need to be very clear to you, because they were not when you were a child. If you grew up with chaos, if the whole family structure broke down and no one was in charge anymore, not the parent or the child, if your home was one of total disorder, then control will be even more important to you.

The needs for clearly defined roles and tight control often come together. You will want your home "just so." And your children "just so." You will want everything very exactly the way you want it. Knowing when to control and when to let go will be especially difficult for you. Allowing your children to make mistakes when you know better will be very painful. For the child, having the opportunity to make the mistake may be more beneficial to her development than doing it "right" would be. Letting the child make mistakes and learn a better way, including the whys and hows, offers more to that child than having her "do it right" because that's the way it's done.

There are times when you will have to keep your thoughts to yourself. There are times when contributing your own thoughts will violate your child's right to have her own thoughts.

There are consequences for children who aren't allowed to make mistakes and have to be perfect all the time. The Japanese educational system exerts very challenging standards of academic excellence on its students. If the students do not meet these standards, movement upward in society becomes very difficult for them. As a result, there is a very high incidence of suicide among young people in Japan. When children are unable to meet the pressure, they opt out the only way they know how. This can be the final result of violating that boundary.

I know a man who always has a "suggestion" of a better way. It can be directions to a restaurant, or an easier way to do homework or that the flame is too high. I can't get it through his head that his children would be so grateful if he would let them feel that their way was good enough—just once.

What happens is that as soon as he starts to say anything, his children turn him off. "All I want to do is help" is his constant cry. Yes, but his need to help is an intrusion on someone else's need to try it their way. It is a boundary violation. When safety is involved or irreparable damage to something valued, it may make sense to intrude anyway. Otherwise, try to butt out. Let your children know you're available to help and stop there.

Controlling kids' thoughts doesn't allow them to develop their creativity. Instead, their minds get filled with ways to preserve whatever they perceive to be the prevailing order and status quo in order not to be violated and criticized. As a result, controlling kids' thoughts may result in your raising either a very repressed child with stomach problems or a child who will one day go out and dye his hair orange and pierce his nose.

You are entitled to your thoughts, and your children are entitled to theirs. All of you do not have to see things in the same way. When you were growing up, you may have been ridiculed or put down or had your reality denied. These family attitudes made it very difficult for you to assert yourself. In order for you to belong in your family you had to think their way. You may have had to keep your thoughts to yourself and you may have questioned your own reality. You received no validation for your thoughts and opinions. You spent time wondering and worrying if there was something wrong with you because you thought and saw things differently from the rest of your family.

At different stages of their development, your children will voice ideas that don't make a lot of sense to you, but certainly do to them.

You will need to listen and validate their right to their thoughts. You may not think peanut butter and mayonnaise is the best sandwich in the world. You may not think their teacher doesn't know anything. You may not want to give up grapes because of the way migrant workers are treated. You may not want to devote your life to saving the whales. You may not think organized religion is stupid, and on and on.

Validating your child's right to her own thoughts does not mean you are not allowed your own point of view. I usually ask a lot of questions. I also express my point of view. When I hear ideas about things that are different than mine, I take the opportunity to encourage the dialogue and the mental exercise. It is my belief that learning how to have a conversation is more important than its content. I demand my right to my belief system and I offer the same right. (Actions and beliefs are different. I will not get in the way of you believing organized religion is passé. But I may still insist you join the family in church on Sunday.)

Simply expressed, your thoughts and those of your children are worthy of respect. If you respect your child's point of view you stand a better chance of making your point. I have vivid memories of an impassioned speech one of my kids made about what a *&@&$#$ the guidance counselor was and just exactly what he was going to tell her. It was time someone did, and on and on and example after example. . . .

My response was simple: "You are probably right [absolutely validating his position], but there are two things you need to keep in mind. One, she already graduated from high school, and two, she has the power to block your graduation."

My thoughts were sobering to him. He had not been denied

his point of view and he decided it would be wiser to go lift weights to work off his frustration rather than self-destruct.

2. CHILDREN HAVE A RIGHT TO THEIR OWN FEELINGS.

"I hate Uncle Manny!" a three-year-old girl screams. You may be tempted out of your own background to say, "I don't want to hear you talk like that. He's my brother and you say only nice things . . ."

That response denies the child the right to her feelings. She decides she is bad, and since your approval makes her feel safe in her world she will deny her feelings and go along with yours. As an adult, this child will put up with more than she needs to and not know when to say "Enough." Adults like these are prone to physical symptoms. They will withstand more than they need to emotionally. They will allow others to take advantage of them, because it's what they were taught and what they know.

They don't know how to stand up for themselves and they also will not have the tools they need to confront someone else. As a result they will say nothing at all or let things build up until they explode. Either way creates new problems but doesn't solve the old ones. So often, if you don't have the tools to do something, you may not even know something can be done. The only way these people are able to make changes in their lives is when they become enraged or sick. Neither of these options is a desirable one. Becoming enraged hurts other people, and becoming sick hurts oneself.

If instead of denying this child's feelings, you say, "You sound angry. How come?" she may tell you that whenever Uncle Manny comes over he makes her sit in his lap and he puts his hand in her underpants and pinches her tush.

Certainly you now have a whole lot more to deal with than if you had disallowed her feelings. But you also stand a better chance of raising an emotionally healthy child. Because they squashed your feelings, your parents did not have to deal with the consequences of them. Hopefully, you are making a different choice.

In many troubled families, feelings are either enmeshed or disengaged. The whole family denies, enables, represses anger, or sets all feelings aside. You took your cue from the others, so it was hard to know whose feelings you were feeling or even *if* you were feeling.

As a child Gail hated her Aunt Edith because her mother hated her and told Gail that Aunt Edith was vicious and nasty and that Gail needed to be careful of her. It wasn't until after Gail's mother died and she got to spend some time with her Aunt Edith that she realized what a sweet lady she was, and that she had hated Aunt Edith not because she had any reason to hate her, but because that's what was done in Gail's family. Gail came to realize her mother might have had her reasons for hating Edith, but that her mother's reasons weren't Gail's reasons.

Your children are entitled to their feelings and to be able to express their feelings. "You shouldn't feel that way!" is an inappropriate response. "I'm sorry you feel that way, because I see it this way" is a much better one.

3. CHILDREN HAVE A RIGHT TO THEIR OWN POSSESSIONS.

Harriet said to me, "When my daughter outgrows her clothes I give them to her cousin, Trina. Trina is thrilled to have them and is most grateful. My daughter resents this bitterly and I can't tolerate her selfishness. After all, I paid for them in the first place."

Taking the clothes without her daughter's permission is a clear violation of Harriet's daughter's boundaries. The violation will cause the child to resent her mother and will make any relationship with her cousin impossible.

Harriet and her daughter had never discussed giving away the clothes. She had never asked her daughter if she minded or if she wanted to be the one to give them away. The practical considerations outweighed everything else. But Harriet couldn't get past these and had no trust in her daughter's judgment on the matter.

It is important that you respect your children's right to their own things. It is important that the child feels some sense of control in her world. If you don't want to share your doll with Jenny, put it away and find something else you are willing to share.

Theresa and Margaret were very competitive sisters who felt insecure about their family's affection for them. Both very appearance-conscious, a focus that had been encouraged by their traditional Irish family, the sisters were always raiding each other's closets for clothing, and even as young adults each accused the other of stealing from her. Their mother had had hypervigilant parents, and as a reaction was very permissive about the sisters' relationship and about boundaries in general, deciding from early childhood that her kids could work things out between themselves without the suffocating interference she had had.

Theresa went away to college and was assigned a roommate named Leslie. Within a month or so, Leslie and Theresa became good friends. About the same time, a disconcerting thing began to happen. Leslie would come home and find Theresa wearing her clothing or jewelry. Once she even came back and found Theresa and her boyfriend kissing on her bed. Leslie told Theresa this behavior made her uncomfortable and that her things were her things. Leslie's attitude was confusing to Theresa, and she found Leslie's need to clarify her boundaries punitive. Soon Theresa cooled to her, and Leslie started to hear that Theresa was speaking badly about her to other people. But the closet-raiding continued. Old patterns are hard to break, especially when the reasons to change them don't make sense. Finally Leslie gave up and requested and received a room transfer.

As a part of the transfer process, both Leslie and Theresa were required to see a dorm supervisor. When Theresa told the supervisor her story, she expressed great hurt and sadness that Leslie, this wonderful friend, could have turned out to be such a cold and selfish person. Meanwhile, Leslie expressed regret that as a result of not wanting to share her possessions without being asked, Theresa thought she did not care for her, because that was not true. She also understood Theresa had meant no harm, that from what Theresa had told Leslie about her relationship with Margaret, this kind of behavior was all Theresa knew. The point was that Leslie did not have the time or the energy to spend all day laying down boundaries with Theresa, and also did not feel she had to.

Regardless of whether or not Theresa can understand Leslie's point of view, she should ask for and respect Leslie's ground rules about her own possessions. The fact that Leslie understands Theresa's history does not make Theresa's behavior acceptable. Because there were no boundaries set in her family, Theresa will have difficulty with people who desire separateness.

Children also collect things. You may insist the rock collection not be kept on the kitchen table, but throwing the rock collection out to teach a child a lesson is devastating. I know a man in his fifties who still resents his mother for throwing away his comic books when he left for camp. It was a profound trust violation.

It may have been that when you were growing up, your things were not respected. Your siblings would wear your clothes or take your toys without even asking. You would have to carefully hide anything you valued and even then you couldn't be sure. You knew if you expressed your feelings you'd be put down for being selfish and unwilling to share. Somehow it would turn around and you'd be the one in trouble. It may be that you too did not respect others' possessions. After all, why should you? They didn't respect yours.

Be sure when your children trade clothes or other possessions that they do so by choice. And make sure they have the freedom to say no.

4. Children have a right to their own space.

In a recent seminar on parenting, a young mother expressed concern: "When I looked in on my four-year-old son when he was taking his bath, he was letting the water hit him 'there'! Is that normal?"

She was confused by my response. "Yes, what he was doing is perfectly normal, but what I'm having a problem with is you invading his privacy."

When this mother was growing up, no one had any privacy. It was not unusual for her parents to walk in on her when she was taking a bath or using the toilet. Her private things were gone into without permission, and if she objected when she saw a sibling wearing her clothes, she was told she was selfish and needed to learn to share.

When she realized this, she said, "Oh my G-d, I remember how awful I felt and I swore I'd be different, and here I am doing the same thing and I wasn't even aware."

Awareness is the first step toward change. Once you are aware you can then learn how to be different. It is not unusual for a child growing up in a dysfunctional family to have his privacy invaded. In these families a closed door to the bedroom or bathroom has no meaning. Private thoughts are invaded: "If you love me, you will tell me everything." Mail is opened, telephone calls are listened to, and secret diaries are read with impunity. Children are made to believe they are doing something wrong if they want to keep a part of themselves to themselves. The child comes to feel like a possession and not a person.

If this was your childhood, it is important not to make the same mistake. You can knock on the child's door just as you ask the child to knock on yours.

Certainly the privacy you give a two-year-old is different than the privacy you give a ten-year-old. But the principle is the same. A child needs his own space, as we all do. Children love to have secret codes and secret languages and the like. These are not designed to exclude you. They are designed to make them feel special and connected to each other. They are a part of growing up.

I hear grown men fondly reminiscing about the secret decoder rings they had as children. I don't think the secrets they shared violated any national or foreign policy, but then again, I didn't have one.

When I was a kid we had a secret language where we put the sound *ob* in front of every vowel. To tell you the truth, we got pretty good at it, and I got a big kick out of it when my own children developed the identical secret language. It is a part of growing up. If you didn't have privacy in your growing up it may be hard for you to respect it, but it is necessary for you to bite the bullet and not violate the boundary.

A child's sense of belonging and security can also be tied up symbolically with his physical space and privacy.

Karl, a very self-reliant businessman with no children, relates: "I was the oldest of seven children. The other six were much younger than I was, and my parents, who were both alcoholic, didn't have very much money or a big house. But I'll still never forget the day after I moved into the college dorm across town. I came home twenty-four hours after I moved out and found that the bedroom I'd had all my life was just gone. Two of my brothers had moved in and already made it their own. All of my things had vanished. No one had told me this was going to happen. I just came in and it was done. And at eighteen I realized I would never be able to really go home again. I felt rootless. They didn't understand why I got so upset. After all, it really wasn't my home anymore. I was treated so coldly for feeling bad about it."

What happened to Karl happens all the time. Parents often make the mistake of not recognizing how difficult life transitions are for their children. And ironically, they often decide to wait for a transition in a child's life to make another such change of their own. For instance, many couples wait to divorce until the last child leaves for college, but that child is devastated because it means her whole life changes and she no longer has an anchor. Changing a child's room without preparing the child for it throws her off. You have the right to do it, because it's your house. But don't assume your child won't have feelings about it. It seems only fair to discuss it so the child can take pleasure in "giving up" rather than feeling replaced.

When my parents sold my childhood home I was very upset, and I was already married with a house and children of my own. My husband said, "But you're living with me now." And I said, "Yeah, but . . ." The difference between the functional and the dysfunctional family here is that in the functional family you have a right to your process, a right to grieve the change. In the dysfunctional family you are called selfish for having these feelings, so you end up feeling like a bad person. In adulthood, children like these will have difficulty trusting people and will be very possessive.

5. CHILDREN HAVE A RIGHT TO THEIR OWN BODIES.

Emily shares, "When I was ten I agreed to meet the school custodian at the basement level of our old school building. A classmate of mine said that was where he gave kids dimes. Wow, I thought! What I didn't know was that he was going to walk me into a bathroom stall, close the door, and molest me.

"He asked me if I liked his hands between my legs and I said, 'I want to go.' I wouldn't take the dime he offered. Later that day he offered me a quarter if I wouldn't tell anyone what had happened.

"Well, I told . . . I told my girlfriend, who told her mother, who called my mother, who did *nothing* except tell me 'to stay away from him.' "

Not only did the school custodian violate Emily's personal boundaries, what he did was illegal. Her mother's minimizing of what happened confused her and further victimized her. Children need their parents to make them feel safe. They also need them to advocate for them.

Your physical boundaries may have been violated in other ways. You may have been bathed by a parent long after you wanted to do it by yourself. You may have been touched when you didn't want to be touched in ways that made you feel dirty. You also may not have had any choice about being hugged or being dressed. All these were violations of your boundaries.

This is very critical. If your child does not want to be hugged, it is his right. Children go through stages. At some stages they love to be held and at others they don't. That needs to be up to them. Not wanting to hold your hand crossing a busy street does not fall into this category. Not wanting to give Auntie Jane a big hug and a kiss does.

Many parents who were molested as children will tend toward repeating the pattern. Others are so fearful of crossing those lines that they deny themselves even appropriate physical contact with their children. They worry about crossing the fine line between being close to and being too intimate with their children. They worry about comfortable levels of undress and inappropriate exposure. They worry about the difference between complimenting a child on his or her appearance and being seductive. If you grew up in a household where the boundaries were unclear and the relationships were unclear, you too may have difficulty knowing what is appropriate.

Without an understanding of what normal psychosexual development is all about, it is easy to develop shame around natural impulses.

Babies explore their bodies and find it pleasurable. The injunctions "You will go blind if you masturbate" or "It will grow hair on your hands," make children unsettled. Explaining to children that some things are to be done in privacy gives a healthier message.

When children reach puberty and see their parents as sexual, and if they don't know that wanting your parent for your lover is a natural part of growing up, they can develop shame to the degree that they identify with those who have experienced incest: "I have no memory of sexual abuse, but I identify with the feelings of shame."

When parents become aware of the change in the body of a

child and the child is sexually naive and still runs around scantily dressed or still wants to sit on Daddy's lap, the father may panic at his impulses and push the child away. The child feels rejected: "My daddy loved me until I became a woman and then he pulled away from me. What's wrong with me?"

Nothing is wrong, of course. Clearly, it is inappropriate to be involved with your children in a way that is potentially sexually arousing to you. But without an understanding of psychosexual development, the father sees himself as a "dirty old man" and the child feels that she has become unlovable. In fact, the child needs to be told that she has an adult body and that the rules have to change.

Overt sexual behaviors that violate boundaries and constitute sexual abuse include inappropriate nudity. For example, an adult walking around the house without any clothes on or an adult standing in the doorway of a child's room unannounced in an attempt to catch the child in the process of getting undressed or being undressed is abusive. It is an invasion of boundaries. Kissing a child on the lips in a lingering way reserved for adult relationships and fondling the child's genital areas are abusive. Masturbating in front of the child, using the child to assist in masturbation, or masturbating the child is abusive. Oral involvement with a child of either sex is abusive, whether it is done to the child or the child is forced to engage in it with the adult. Putting a finger or a penis or other object into the child's anus or vagina is abusive. Dry intercourse is another example of abusive behavior.

If any of what has been discussed here relates to you, SEEK PROFESSIONAL HELP IMMEDIATELY. The damage you will do to your child—even if you believe it feels good—is most serious. (Much of this discussion is taken from my book *Healing Your Sexual Self*. I suggest you read it to gain a fuller understanding of the implications.)

Finally, remember that parents have boundaries, too. When you feel suffocated or you feel stifled or you feel invaded, that means *your* boundaries have been violated. Wondering whether or not you have the right to feel this way is not the measure of whether or not your boundary has been breached. Your child bursting into your room with a bloody nose as you are trying to have ten quiet minutes alone after a busy day is a violation of your space. Unfortunately, when you are a parent, you sometimes have to permit violations of your own space. The child's need must come first.

But your children also feel suffocated or stifled and invaded, and attention needs to be paid to that as well. As you become more tuned in to your own boundaries, it will become easier to automatically respect those of your children.

S I X

TOLERATING FEELINGS

---

a) *In a healthy family all feelings are tolerated.*

b) *In an unhealthy family feelings are often violated and are therefore repressed.*

Tonya says, "When I was a child I would lie in my bed night after night in terror listening to my parents fight. I was so scared one of them would get killed. Sometimes I got so hysterical that I ran downstairs and begged them to stop. It didn't make any difference. It was like I was invisible.

"As an adult I cannot tolerate conflict of any kind. When my children fight I freak out. And I will do anything to keep the peace in my marriage.

"I know I am overreacting because of my childhood, but the feelings come up so fast they wash over me. I feel powerless to respond any other way.

"I know I am teaching my children that their feelings are not okay with me, and this is something I need to work on."

If your emotional reaction to a situation is bigger than it

needs to be, chances are that you too are reacting to something other than what has just happened. Chances are, your feelings have to do with something else.

Susan reports, "When I walk into my house and the kitchen is in disarray, I take it as a personal affront. I'm outraged. The response of my kids is always the same. 'What's the big deal? In five minutes I was "gonna." ' These responses don't make me feel any better at all. Every fiber in my body tenses. As they get older my children make more of an attempt to keep me from walking into chaos, not because they believe it makes sense to, but because they don't want to upset me. Frankly, that's reason enough as far as I'm concerned.

"My reaction is a result of my own history. I used to joke about my mother and her white glove, but I'm certain on a deep level I believe that the fact that my house is not immaculate is a negative reflection on me. My mother is deceased now, but whenever she came to visit I would take pains to have the house and everyone in it whipped into shape. I found no humor at all in the situation, and whispers of 'Watch out—Granny's coming' were not funny to me. But if the truth be told, there really was no way to satisfy my mother. She would always find something out of place. It was inevitable."

Susan's overreaction does not mean children should not learn to clean up after themselves or that they shouldn't be told to return to do it if they haven't. But it is also perfectly fine for them to decide you're unreasonable if you interrupt whatever else they're doing or, G-d forbid, ask them to also put away a dish they didn't mess.

To repress these sentiments would be to repress their own feelings, which are perfectly natural. Kids are sloppy by nature. Kids create havoc, and that's their job. Parents try to get them to clean up, and that's their job. So there's nothing wrong with being angry if the house is a mess and there's nothing wrong with being annoyed when you are pressed to clean up after yourself. Nothing is in question here but anger on the part of the parent that seems out of proportion to the situation, and as a result, kids repressing their annoyed feelings because they are afraid. This pattern is one that will lead to your kids being repressed the way you were as a child. It leads to kids believing there is something inherently wrong with them other than the fact that they're kids.

All I am saying here is that a child's sloppiness is not a capital crime. Making sure children help out with the household is one of the chores of parenting. You need to be able to recognize this and behave on the basis of what is going on in the moment in the real world and not to react to your own childhood. Otherwise, you will be encouraging your children to repress healthy feelings.

Can you think of examples of situations in your own parenting life where you tend to overreact? The examples may relate to:

- Cleanliness of the child or house
- Your need to be in control
- Your child's school performance
- Sibling spats
- Your child's popularity
- Your child's physical appearance
- Your child's whining

Ellen came to see me for counseling because her adolescent daughter had just gained a lot of weight. Ellen saw herself at that age in her daughter and was repulsed by her. She knew she had to do something about this so the child wouldn't pick up her feelings and be shamed. When Harold's son got a B in Science you would have thought the world had come to an end. Since Harold had planned for his son to be an engineer before he was born, this was a crushing blow to his fatherly ego. The boy was treated as if he were a failure.

The time to begin to practice sorting this out is a quiet, reflective time, not when you're caught up in it. At that time the feelings are too big for you to separate them out. The enormity of the impact on you is the clue that you are reacting more to the past than the present. If you have given thought to this subject ahead of time, you may be able to recognize the difference between an appropriate reaction and an inappropriate reaction.

A child needs to learn how to express and deal with feelings. If his feelings are not responded to in a way that is validating, those feelings will go underground.

In Mike's family getting angry only made things worse: "If I let them see me happy they'd spoil it. If I cried they'd give me something to cry about. And the thought of letting them know I'm scared really scared me.

"As a result I'm not real good at expressing my feelings, and even though I know that expressing them is a good idea, I still don't know how to identify them and work them through."

It may be that you automatically push feelings down when they start to surface. Mike is very upset that his son never seems to show any emotion. Mike related to me that he had recently spoken to his mother, whose best friend had just died. Mike was upset that his mother hadn't seemed to be the least disturbed by this news.

"Now I know where Tom gets it from," he said.

"Oh, no," I said. "That may be where *you* get it from but you are *his* role model."

When Ginny brought home straight A's she just laid her report card on the kitchen counter without saying a word. She felt no pride or excitement in her report card, because straight A's were what her parents always expected she would get. As a result, her achievement had no meaning. The one time Ginny got a B, she tried to erase it from the page.

A man once told me that when he was growing up he felt like the librarian in the orchestra. The librarian in the orchestra is the one who is in charge of putting the music on the stands for the musicians. If he does his job correctly, no one is even aware there is such a job. If he makes a mistake, no matter how small, there is havoc.

Children do not start out repressed. They cry, they yell, they are startled, they giggle automatically. Expressing feelings is not something you have to teach them. The teaching is in allowing and validating the expression of feelings and in showing where and how to express them.

Feelings will generally fall into four general categories: *mad, sad, glad,* and *scared.* There are variations on each theme. Validate your child's feelings and his right to them. Respond, don't ignore.

Child: "I hate Jimmy."

Parent: "You sound angry. What's happening?"

Child: "My goldfish is dead. I'm so miserable."

Parent: "Would you feel better if we had a funeral?"

Child: "This is the best hot dog in the whole world!"

Parent: "I'm glad you like it."

Child: "There is a monster in my closet."

Parent: "Let me check to be sure there's nothing here. I want you to feel safe."

Your own feelings may have been so repressed you can't even identify with them. The following list from my book *Lifeskills for Adult Children* will help you put words to feelings. As you practice you will become more sensitive to the nuances within each feeling. It will be useful if you start recognizing what goes on inside of you. That will help you encourage your children to be forthcoming.

SAD	MAD	GLAD	SCARED
ashamed	angry	blissful	afraid
bored	annoyed	calm	anxious
depressed	disgusted	cheerful	concerned

discouraged	distraught	comfortable	confused
embarrassed	frustrated	confident	insecure
guilty	irritated	encouraged	nervous
helpless	jealous	excited	panicky
hurt	offended	fulfilled	shocked
lonely	resentful	happy	tense
regretful		loving	terrified
sickened		overjoyed	uncertain
tired		passionate	
uncomfortable		pleased	
unhappy		relieved	
weary			

Play a game with your family. See if you can use each of these feeling words in a sentence and try and demonstrate the feelings as you say the sentence. For example: "I felt *guilty* when I ate the last piece of cake even though I knew you wanted it." "I feel *encouraged* that you like my idea."

If feelings are not expressed appropriately, they either go underground or get distorted.

They get rationalized: "I didn't want to go to the party anyway."

They get projected: "I know you never liked me."

They get repressed: "I really have no feelings about that."

They get displaced: When Harry's wife told him what a rotten husband he was, he kept his feelings to himself. When he got to the office he thought he had put it aside. But pretty soon, without real provocation, he found himself shouting, "Why can't anyone do a decent job around here?"

Your brain makes a decision to displace your feelings. However, your body doesn't get fooled. Feelings that are not expressed either get imploded or exploded. If they get imploded you (or your children) will somatize. This means that you will develop physical symptoms. These can include the whole range of gastrointestinal problems, skin rashes, and breathing problems, to name a few. Stress-related illnesses result largely from repressed feelings.

Angry feelings that get exploded surface as rage, which is an out-of-control stage. Rage gets expressed in various forms of violence and tantrums. Angry feelings that get imploded often show up as depression. This is demonstrated largely in withdrawal and constant sadness.

Feelings unexpressed or expressed inappropriately create new problems and complicate old ones.

This encourages inappropriate behavior in children.

Jeanie broke the kitchen chair and was afraid to tell her mother. This behavior is typical of a child. When Jeanie's mother saw the broken chair she fired the housekeeper. The little girl felt very guilty and told her mother the truth. The mother, who was unable to admit ever doing anything wrong, refused to believe the child. This led to a lot of confusion on the part of the child and brought the child's reality into question, because her mother was saying that what she believed could not be so.

Encourage your children to talk about how they feel. Discourage acting out, but talking about what they would like to say or do is fine. Sometimes physical exercise is a good idea or sometimes just being held as they cry. All those things you needed when you were a child but couldn't ask for because it would only make matters worse, you can now offer to your own children. How fortunate for them.

Children are not short adults and react differently to things than adults do. Their perspective is directly related to their life experience and it is important to keep that in mind.

I remember trying to console a little child when his grandfather died. I said to him, "We will both miss your grampa, but don't forget that he lived a long life and was eighty-five years old when he died." Unimpressed, the child turned to me and said, "I know that, but I only knew him for seven!"

THE PARENT AS TEACHER
AND GUIDE

a) In a healthy family the parent is a teacher and guide.

b) In an unhealthy family the children bring themselves up the best they can.

SEVERAL MONTHS AGO my daughter told me she was about to attend a workshop on dressing well on a budget. She would learn how to accessorize her clothing and, in effect, make eighteen outfits out of eight. I said to her, "That's a great idea. By the way, there is something I never learned about wearing scarves that I always wanted to know. There is a question I would like you to ask your teacher for me."

She replied, "Tell me what it is, because if you don't know, I certainly don't!"

Perfect parenting is a myth. There is simply no such thing.

Not only doesn't it exist, it is not even desirable. Parents are people. They are human. They make mistakes. They also can't know everything.

Responsible parenting is not a myth. It is the child's birthright. Owning up to mistakes or not having the answer is part of modeling appropriate, acceptable parental behavior. Trying to correct mistakes and helping to discover the answer is another part.

If you grew up in a family where one parent was addicted and the other parent was addicted to the parent who was addicted; or where there was only one parent, who was totally overwhelmed by all the responsibilities; or where all the answers to every question were written in stone; or in any other home where there was no time or energy to answer your many questions, you simply learned how not to ask. You learned you were a nuisance if you asked and you wouldn't get answers that made sense to you anyway. So if you did ask, you were ignored, abused, or made to feel guilty that you had added to the burden of an already overwhelmed parent. You stopped asking questions. Your questions were stupid anyway.

As a result you grew up without a data base for life. You learned much in school, but no one answered the more fundamental questions involved in everyday life. No one taught you how to get along in this world.

School can do just so much. There are several areas where it is up to the parent to educate the child. It is up to the parent to open his children's minds to exploring new ideas and experiences and also to educate children about their heritage. This education at home not only provides the child with valuable information and approaches for living, but also provides basic building blocks of identity that she can later use to fashion individual approaches and solutions of her own in untested life situations.

Two mothers had to provide cookies for a bake sale benefiting their kids' intramural soccer league. Both mothers were single, held demanding full-time jobs, and had many other family obligations. Evelyn didn't want her kid to feel different from the other kids. She came up with a plan. On the way home from the office, she stopped by a local bakery and purchased a couple of pounds of delicious cookies, which she then took home, re-wrapped in her own container, and presented to her delighted daughter Jennifer over breakfast the next morning, with no one the wiser. Jocelyn, on the other hand, was panicked at the idea of baking something for her son Barry to donate. She didn't know when she would find the time. Irritated, she rebuffed his nudging, which clearly came from his fear of being criticized by the other kids for not bringing something to the bake sale. Jo-celyn's guilt grew and grew, and indeed she finally did think of something. At eleven o'clock on the night before the bake sale, after all the children were in bed and all the chores and all the preparation for her office presentation on the next day were done, Jocelyn began to bake with a vengeance, and from scratch.

Jocelyn slept very little that night. She knew she would be tired for her presentation. But in the morning when Barry got up the kitchen was sparkling once again and a package of dozens of perfect sugar cookies awaited him. Jocelyn had really outdone herself. When Barry came home that night, he announced to his exhausted and guilt-ridden mother that his cookies were the best and all his friends thought she was perfect.

Years later, Evelyn recounted the story of the buying-the-cookies-and-repackaging-them routine to a group of other women at a bridal shower for a friend's daughter. Her story was greeted with much laughter, as other working mothers revealed they had resorted to the same secret baking method when their kids were younger.

Jocelyn was at the shower, too. But she wasn't laughing. She was astonished. First she felt angry. Then she felt foolish. Finally, she shook her head and laughed at herself. "Why didn't I think of that?" Jocelyn asked. "I thought I had to knock myself out to be perfect. Now, I know better."

Several other women in the room nodded their heads, and they recounted similar stories of their own.

Evelyn came from a functional family system. She had access to an extensive data base and felt confident about her parenting abilities. She used her building blocks to come up with a new, personalized solution that was "okay."

Jocelyn came from a troubled family. She knew the final result she wanted—she'd seen it in magazines, on television, and in other people's families. But she didn't have enough confidence in her parenting abilities or the building blocks she needed to come up with a solution that was appropriate to her unique situation. For Jocelyn, the bake sale represented a situation that was out of control. So instead of managing it, she was very absent-minded and laissez-faire about it, rebuffing her son's concerns until the last minute, when she exhausted herself alleviating them.

Teaching children about family culture and traditions, social skills, appreciation of literature and the arts, and respect of ethnic groups vastly contributes to a child's data base for life, along with the other parenting skills described in this book. Such a data base teaches skills that will allow your children not only to participate in traditions, but also gives them a strong sense of self and provides them with data to draw on to make individualistic and appropriate decisions as they approach unique or challenging situations in their lives.

Children need to know about their family culture. This is part of their data base. They need to know what it means to be Italian or Irish or African-American. They need to know the family rituals that express their culture, and they also need to know their cultural history. This helps to give the child a sense of belonging and roots. It gives the child a sense of ethnic identity. It is a part of who the child is.

Several years ago I worked with a small Native American tribe in Alaska. These Native Americans had a terrible problem with alcoholism and desperately wanted to impact positively on the next generation in this regard. They had hired many consultants before me, and the consultants had come in and told them what they were doing wrong, how they had to change, and left. The Native Americans attempted to put these things into practice, but they didn't work. They actually ended up much more confused than they had been before and began to lose a sense of their identity. When I sat with them I told them to talk with the elders in the community and to write down the lore that had been passed down from generation to generation. This was precious material that would otherwise be lost forever. If the new generation didn't have a sense of their history and an appreciation of it, they would have less to hang on to and be less rooted. Diseases such as alcoholism thrive where there is ethnic confusion.

Often, rituals end up in an individual family's culture or history without anyone ever questioning them. If your parents or other relatives are still alive, ask questions about your own family traditions. Encourage your children to ask you questions. What you learn about yourselves and each other can be quite remarkable.

A woman I know tells the following story:

"Every Easter we have a ham dinner at my mom's and my mom cuts the ham in two before she puts it in the oven. I was familiar with this ritual and never paid it much mind. Then one year my five-year-old said to me, 'Mom, why does Grandma cut the ham in two pieces before she puts it in the oven?' My response was, 'I have no idea. We've always just done that in our family.' So I asked my mother, 'Why do you always cut the ham in two before you put it in the oven?' And *she* said, 'I have no idea. We've always just done that in our family.'

"We were fortunate in that the fourth generation was still alive. Not only my mother but my grandmother was present that Easter. 'Grandma,' I said, 'why do we always cut the ham in two before we put it in the oven?' She replied, 'Because I never had a pan large enough to hold the whole ham. I had no choice!' "

That story will remain in the annals of that family's culture for years to come. It is a wonderfully warm example of how things get passed down from generation to generation without question. The answer to the question, when it was finally asked, told everyone something about resourcefulness and creative problem solving, important data base skills, and also about the rewards of asking questions.

Children also need to know about their family's religious identity. They need to know what it means to be Catholic or Jewish or Baptist. They need to be exposed to the values their family's religion expresses and to their implications. The ceremonies surrounding Baptism, Confirmation, or Bar Mitzvah all confer a sense of belonging and identity on a child. The family rituals of seder at Passover for Jewish families or the midnight mass before Christmas for Catholic families also give the child a sense of belonging.

Having the benefit of a data base like the one a religious identity provides also gives children the ability to make their own choices about religion when they reach adulthood. They will be able to maintain, revise, or exchange this identity for another that may suit their individuality and circumstances more precisely at that time. In short, they will have access to an important building block they can use to build the foundation of their choice for themselves and their own children.

Home is also where children learn how to treat other people. It is critical that while we teach ethnic pride and religious identity we do not lose sight of the family of man. Bigotry begins at home. A child does not perceive a different race or accent as inferior without direction from her parents. Hate is learned.

We teach our children not to accept rides from strangers, not to walk alone in dark streets at night, not to wander into bad neighborhoods, not to leave possessions unattended. The risks to their person and possessions exist, unfortunately, but unsavory people are not linked to any particular racial or ethnic group. This has to be made clear to children. But first, we need to believe it ourselves.

We come to believe it ourselves through the way we live our lives. Children learn appreciation of cultural differences—instead of fear of or prejudice against cultural differences—through the behavior of their parents.

A black client of mine was getting married to a white woman. His family had disowned him and would not acknowledge his marriage. He asked me to stand up for him, and I proudly did so. As the guests filed by on the receiving line after the ceremony and shook my hand, I said, "Hi! I'm Jan. I'm the groom's mom." When they looked at me a little strangely, I smiled and simply said, "I know I look too young to be his mother."

Having grown up in this climate, my own children are not afraid to acknowledge the differences in people, but at the same time relate to the specialness in all people.

To experience the specialness of all people is one of the great values of living in the United States. Not everyone in the world has the opportunity to savor such a diverse ethnic mix. It always bothers me when people say, "I didn't even notice you were Asian," or, "I barely remember you are African-American." Sometimes, I think people mistakenly believe that statements like these announce they don't have a bias. But noticing the differences in people does not indicate a bias. It indicates your eyes are open. And to pretend differences do not exist confuses children. It's making judgments about differences between people that you want to avoid.

Home is also where children learn their social skills. You cannot learn how to carry on a conversation if you are not taught how to do so. You can't learn to be comfortable in social situations if no one ever listened to what you had to say. Home is where you learn how to do this.

One of the ways you as a parent can help in this regard is to answer all of your child's questions, no matter how irrelevant they may seem:

"Why can't I when Johnny's mother let him?"
"What should I do about . . . ?"
"Why?" "Why?" "What?" "What?"
"How do I look?"
"Can we . . . ?"
—and on and on.

Answers like "Because I said so" do not further the child's data base. It may solve your problems for the moment, but if the reason you gave that answer had to do with your instincts telling you your answer made sense and you don't know why, take the time to discover the answer with your child. Chances are, you are right, but that is not good enough. You need to look the answer up or reason it out together or with someone else. Not only does this answer the question, but it teaches the child an approach to life. It teaches children that if you do not understand something you are told, it is appropriate to continue to ask questions until you know the answer.

It is also up to parents to impart a sense of wonder and respect of nature to their children. It is up to parents to teach children an appreciation of our environment and the risks to it. Our children's lives will be directly influenced by the environment. The children on our block made sure none of the neighbors burned their leaves because burning leaves is bad for the environment, and aerosol spray cans are no longer allowed in our homes.

This is an area that is all too easy for adults with busy lives to neglect. Do *you* stop to smell the roses? Watching the change of seasons and the life cycle or learning about caring for a small animal can be a valuable shared experience.

Parents can also give their children the opportunity to appreciate literature and music and the arts.

Do you ever think to take your child to a museum or an art show or a concert in the park? These are inexpensive activities that enrich a young life, but if your parents never took you then it may not even occur to you to do this.

Margaret relates, "When I took my kids to see the Alvin Ailey dance company I had the pleasure of listening to my older son Alex explain to my younger son Josh how strong the male dancers had to be to do their job. Alex said the coordination and the strength it took to do the leads and to carry the ballerina were even more difficult than what he was learning in doing sports. This gave Josh an important perspective, because his friends thought dancing was 'sissy stuff.'

"It made me feel really good that Alex could appreciate the dancers that way. Alex also showed Josh that there was more going on than there appeared to be on the surface of things."

This last perception is one that Josh will be able to apply to other life situations, and adds to his data base generally. Since Josh also admired his older brother Alex, he could use Alex as his resource when he spoke to his friends about what he had learned. Alex knew about the strength and training required for dance because his mother began to take him to see cultural events when he was young, and Alex's input further strengthened the family data base.

Although children complain about their music lessons or about practicing for the school orchestra, as adults they are rarely sorry we made them do it. Music lessons or dance lessons or art or any other kind of lessons teach children a certain discipline, which again is transferable to other areas of life and which also gives them pleasure, a source of appreciation, and a way to interact socially with other people.

After a particularly horrific fifth-grade concert, I remember asking a child who it was who was doing all the squeaking. The child turned to me matter-of-factly and said, "We all squeak." The children enjoyed playing in the orchestra and that was all that mattered to them. To them, the "squeaking" was nothing to be defensive about. It was just the way it was.

When Chandra was five years old she would wake up in the middle of the night crying, "I can play it!" At which point she would run down to the piano and play a song she knew by ear. When Chandra was seven, her mother insisted she take piano lessons. Chandra resented the lessons, and for a while she lost her spontaneous ear. Chandra's mother even picked up the phone one day and heard her daughter saying to her piano teacher, "This is Chandra's mother and she can't make her lesson today." Chandra's mother interrupted, and they all had a good laugh over it. Needless to say, the child made her lesson. And now as an adult she's glad she did. Now she can both read music and play songs by ear, and both are very fulfilling to her.

Finally, it is up to parents to teach children the value of honesty and integrity as a way of life.

A dog had been hanging around our house. I assumed it was a neighborhood dog and would eventually return home. I instructed my family not to let the dog in the house and not to feed him. I didn't want to encourage him to continue to hang around.

They didn't let him in the house but they continued to feed him. My son checked the dog's tags and discovered he was not from our neighborhood, but from a distance of several miles away. He called the owners and they arranged to pick up their dog.

My son told me what he had done and I complimented him on his thoughtfulness. He said the people had been frantically searching for days and were very grateful.

"If they offer you a reward, will you take it?" I asked.

"Of course not," he said.

"Why not?"

"Because you brought me up not to accept money for things that people should just do for other people."

These are the moments that make all the effort worth it.

We learn in many ways if we continue to ask questions. Sometimes the answers are surprising.

The greatest reward of teaching and guiding your children is that you continue to learn while you are doing it. Fostering growth in other people enhances you. Everyone benefits. The drive in the country, the piano lesson, the rescued bird, the wallet returned, the flowers sent to the bereaved, these things enrich the lives of all of those involved.

E I G H T

SETTING REASONABLE LIMITS

a) *In a healthy family there are reasonable limits and structure.*

b) *In an unhealthy family there is chaos or extreme rigidity.*

A MAN I KNOW just happened to wake up at five in the morning and looked out his window just in time to see his fifteen-year-old daughter pull his new car out of the driveway. Needless to say, he was enraged.

A phone call to a friend who had "been through it" was a temporizing influence which helped him make the punishment somewhat more realistic. The expression of shock and disbelief on the child's face when she quietly snuck in the house after her little joyride and found her father sitting in the rocker awaiting her return was quite a sight to behold.

Setting and enforcing limits is the job of the parent. Testing and trying to stretch limits is the job of children. It is a perpetual battle and it is as it has to be.

Limits are set for reasons of safety, to determine a structure, to learn appropriate personal and interpersonal boundaries, and to learn right from wrong in terms of civil, moral, and religious law. Setting and defining limits and boundaries teaches children how to live in the world. Setting limits and boundaries also helps children feel secure. Without limits, there is confusion and no sense of what works and what doesn't work. Limits protect boundaries and always relate to discipline. Limits that are too rigid are punishing both for the child and for the adult who enforces them. They also either make a child rebellious or fearful.

The rules themselves vary from family to family and from culture to culture. The goals, however, need to be the same and they need to be consistent.

If you grew up in a dysfunctional family, you are probably very confused at this point. The words may make sense but they have nothing to do with your life experience.

In your childhood, limit setting may have been very inconsistent. A crime that called for severe punishment one day might be ignored the next. Sometimes one of your siblings would get blamed when it was your fault and other times you would get blamed when it was somebody else's fault. If your parent happened to be alcoholic, there were also times when you had no idea at all what you were in trouble about.

As a result, chances are you tried to keep a low profile around the house. The less visible you were the better off you would be. This makes it difficult for you to learn how to determine and enforce limits for your own children now.

Rules should make sense. Children need rules that create structure in their lives. This is the time to get up, to do homework, have dinner, go to bed. When I was growing up, dinner in my house was set for 6:00 P.M. As we got older we began to call in if we couldn't make it. I continue to have that rule in my own house so I know where everyone is at that time. It works for us.

Children will resist bedtime rules and later will resist rules around curfew. Attempting to stretch limits is in their nature. Children need their sleep and their routine. It is in their best interest to have a bedtime—ideally a process which involves slowing down and relaxing first.

Bedtime is one of the predictable struggles between parent and child: "Why do I have to go to bed at seven-thirty when Bobby's mother lets him stay up until eight-thirty?"

You may or may not have an answer. If you don't have the answer you can enter a journey of discovery with your child. When I explored the answers to my children's questions, I was often surprised at what I learned. Yes, maybe the kids were right. They were not ready to go to bed at 7:30. The time was set more for my needs than for theirs. I needed time for myself. Once I had acknowledged that there were many choices and compromises available, things could usually be worked out.

The key for me was that their bedtime was determined at least in part by my need for personal space, so that time became a quiet time in their rooms instead. They didn't "have" to go to sleep. You can't *make* someone go to sleep, but you can tie their stomach up in knots with the pressure.

Children do not necessarily want to win the points they battle for. That is why it is important for you to be on firm ground when you take a position. Offering reasons for a decision puts information in a child's data bank that the child can draw on later when he needs to make decisions on his own.

"Everybody else can" is the child's universal protest. And it goes on in all homes at the same time. The parent who falls for that is taking the path of least resistance and is making the mistake of believing that the child really wants to do what he is fighting tooth and nail for permission to do.

"No," Nancy said to her eight-year-old. "If you and your friends want to see the fireworks, I will take you. You cannot go without a grown-up. If you say Bobby's mother is going, I will call her to be sure. It's not that I don't trust you. It's just that too many folks are careless with firecrackers and I want to know you are safe."

"But . . . but . . . but!!!"

"You have two choices. I can go along or you can stay home. It's up to you."

There was no further protest. The child had needed to save face with his friends. Now satisfied that he had not wimped out, having a parent along didn't seem so terrible after all.

"I'll get killed if I'm not on time" is a refrain that has kept many a kid out of trouble that peer pressure would otherwise have made impossible to resist.

It is up to you to set acceptable parameters of behavior: You do not have my permission to smoke or drink. Disrespectful language is unacceptable in our home. You keep your hands to yourself. You respect the property and privacy of others.

It is up to you to determine family responsibilities. They may include doing the dishes, setting the table, mowing the lawn, going to church, visiting relatives, being courteous to visitors.

It is up to you to determine appropriate dress codes, and standards of personal hygiene and neatness.

Setting limits that have to do with taking care of personal property is a constant stress point between parent and child.

It is entirely possible that if you grew up with anarchy, you did everything you could to keep your little corner of the universe orderly. Chances are that you carried this habit into adulthood. You may even be compulsively neat.

If your children are "normal," the battle of the room is never-ending. It will enrage you. You may find it intolerable. You will still not be able to see the carpet.

The campaign for personal cleanliness without prodding will take a positive turn all by itself about the time hormones start to rage. Throwing left-around clothes and toys into a barrel can keep the place relatively neat. Of course, there are certain things that will never be seen again but all options have their downside.

If the condition of a child's room in and of itself indicates failure as a parent, then we are all failures. It has been suggested that a drain be put in the middle of the floor to flush out children's bedrooms periodically.

Reason does not work. "It is not *your* room. It is a room you have the use of as long as you live in my house!" doesn't work either. Threats don't work. Punishment rarely works.

Bribing and blackmail do work, but only temporarily. A friend of mine, commenting on how immaculate one of her children's rooms was, said, "He must want something *big.*"

Closing the door works. But periodic checks for things nesting or growing is recommended.

I suggest you don't take it personally. And when you're able to accomplish that, let me know *how you did it.*

A consequence that suits the behavior and teaches a lesson is what limit setting is all about.

Sometimes people make up rules because it seems like a good idea at the time. But bear in mind that you will have to live with the consequence of the rule making, which includes enforcement and justification. What may make sense for one day may not make sense the next, and you're stuck with what you do.

A friend of mine had a new sofa delivered for their den. Her husband said, "Are we going to have a rule about eating in the den?"

She thought for a minute and then said, "I don't think so." The children had gotten to be of an age when they no longer messed up whatever they touched. Several years earlier, yes, but not now.

Later that night she and her husband had a good laugh as they sat eating a snack on the new sofa while their son and one of his friends sat at the kitchen table to eat theirs.

So when you're making a rule, make sure you're making an age-appropriate rule. And be flexible about rule making.

I remember refusing to buy one of my sons a new raincoat because he had traded off his good-quality coat at school and come home with garbage.

When I gave him my reasons my son said to me, "Mom, that was five years ago. Chances are, I would need a new raincoat by now even if I hadn't made that mistake."

Disciplining children when they violate limits is a tough job. Some "crimes" carry their own penalty. That window you broke comes out of your allowance or newspaper-route money. If you can't get home when you're due, you're grounded next weekend. Temper tantrums are to be ignored. Begging doesn't work either.

If the crime doesn't carry its own penalty, it becomes your responsibility to be sure there is a consequence for the child's inappropriate behavior. This is one of the most difficult things a parent has to do. Confining a child to his room used to be the way to go, particularly if a child couldn't behave with others, but these days when the child's room is equipped with his TV, computer, phone, and all sorts of other goodies it is harder to think of this as punitive. However, penalties for antisocial behavior do need to involve being separated from the scene of the action.

Listening to children's point of view is also worth it. A willingness to listen doesn't obligate the parent to back down. Your child might say, "If I do the lawn now, I'll be late for the game. I promise I'll do it first thing in the morning." Your listening to arguments and proposals like this one and showing trust in your child's word can help her develop a sense of personal responsibility, which is the goal of limit setting. If the child doesn't follow through on her word, then make a different choice next time.

Needless to say, setting and enforcing limits is a big job. Obviously the nature of the limit setting changes according to the age of the child.

Keep in mind that the limit must make sense to you, and make sure you are willing to take the energy required to enforce it.

When children reach the age of reason, there are ways to make limits clear with less personal aggravation for you. For instance, "I'll drop you off at your friend's as soon as you finish cleaning the kitchen." "I'll take you to the store as soon as your homework is done." This is what you want from me. Well, this is what I want from you.

One advantage of having children who have reached the age of reason is the possibility of making limits clear without going to war over them.

Rachel and her family moved into their new house before the sale was completed on the old one. One afternoon Rachel dropped over to check on the old house and discovered her son had been giving parties in her house that she had not been invited to. On the one hand, Rachel thought her seventeen-year-old, Rob, was very clever. On the other hand, she knew this was not behavior that could go unpunished.

First, she called the police and let them know she had moved and that she had a seventeen-year-old who was possibly using the house as his private retreat. She told them she would appreciate their checking on the house to be sure this was not going on. The police were somewhat amused, but agreed to follow through.

Then Rachel went home and said to Rob, "Remember all of those things you said you had to do that you were not going to have time to do because you had so many plans for the weekend? Amazingly enough, you now have all the time you need. Because you, my dear, are grounded. Would you care to know why?"

"I don't think that's necessary," Rob replied.

And that was the end of that. Rachel didn't have to get enraged, and Rob didn't have to get overly defensive.

Rob wanted to get caught. He was smart enough not to have left the evidence of his parties behind if he didn't choose to. So Rachel's solution provided an important closure for him as well. Getting away with it was not in anyone's best interests. Rob didn't get defensive because Rachel didn't level charges. She asked if he wanted to know why, and he said no. He knew that she knew, and she knew that he knew, and they both knew that the other one knew that they knew, and that was that.

Quite often, chores are connected to a weekly allowance, which makes them a little easier to enforce. Accept the fact that not only will you be met with resistance, but also that, I am convinced, all children share the same secret hope: "I will not do the job the way they want it done and then maybe they won't ask me to do it again." It is not that they can't do anything right—as you believed about yourself—it is that they choose to do it carelessly because they'd rather not bother. The idea is not to berate them for being inept and aggravate yourself, but to let them know they can take whatever time they need in order to do it properly.

Corporal punishment is not acceptable. "My father used to let me have it with a belt and it didn't do me any harm" is not an acceptable rationale for beating your children. Hitting is child abuse. Withdrawal of love is not acceptable either. And instilling fear of abandonment or physical abuse does not teach a child right from wrong, only compliance.

There is no question there are times that parents want to haul off and let kids really have it. These are not unnatural feelings to have. But acting on them is another matter. If you fear you will lose control, that is the time to physically remove yourself from the offending child until you are once again in control. Call Parents Anonymous and have someone talk you down until you are more rational. Then, and only then, address the behavior that made you so angry.

If you are enraged, and that happens to all of us, it is a good idea to wait until you calm down a little. Taking action when you're in such a state may not have the desired result. Fear of your temper is not the best way to keep a child in line. So count to ten or to one hundred if you need to before you react to the behavior.

I caution you against screaming as a habitual form of discipline. You may feel better, but the result will be that your children will turn you off and not hear you at all. I suggest you reserve raising your voice for when a child is in danger and you want an immediate reaction. Examples of this would be when she darts into the street after a ball and a car is coming or when he is about to put something dangerous into his mouth.

One parent should not determine a punishment for the other parent to enforce. You can't ground the kid and expect your wife to stay home to be sure he doesn't go out. Nor can you threaten a child with his father as punishment. "Wait till I tell your father" is destructive to that relationship and does not solve the problem.

If this area boggles you or if you believe your child is out of control, seek help from a professional counselor. That will help you sift out the normal from the extreme and will help you learn how to respond appropriately.

Remember once again that the focus has to be on what is in the best interest of the child. Children's misbehavior will trigger off all sorts of things in you. But responding to their actions out of your own history will not help them to become responsible citizens. Candy's daughter Ellen said to her, "Mom, you were a lousy punisher, but you brought us up to know right from wrong and have a strong inner ethical sense. Therefore, when we did something wrong, we knew we were doing something wrong and we did it on purpose. Now, as adults, we are clear about the difference."

All the difficulties parents face in teaching values and setting limits play themselves out in the area of alcohol and drugs.

Barbara was devastated. Her eighteen-year-old, Sam, had just been picked up for drunken driving.

"It's all my fault," she said. "I knew he was drinking and didn't do anything about it. I just didn't want to face it, so I thought if I didn't make a big deal it would go away. I know about denial from my own alcoholism and now I'm doing it again. Unbelievable."

Sam is out of control. And as difficult as it can be, Barbara has to take charge.

Adolescents believe their friends know better than their parents. Certainly acceptance by their friends is more important than the approval of their parents. However, it is their parents to whom they need be accountable—like it or not.

Many parents feel powerless with respect to their children and drug or alcohol abuse. They are not:

1. You can educate your children about drugs and alcohol. They will also be learning about them in school. You never know what or when something they hear will make a difference.

2. Know who their friends are. Don't be afraid to show up unannounced at a party.

3. If you are fearful that your child is attending a party where alcohol and/or drugs are available, call the police. Let them break up the party.

4. Check with other parents to be sure you get the same story from them.

5. Calling the police and checking with other parents is not something you should keep secret from your children. They need to be told: "I worry about you and I will check up." Once again, they don't have to like it.

6. Have your home be a place where kids can hang out and have plenty of food and soda on hand.

7. Know what your kids do with their free time and be sure they have very little of it.

8. Quite often kids who get involved in athletics care about what they put into their bodies and how they take care of them.

9. Be available to talk to your teenagers about whatever is on their minds. If you are truly available, chances are they will be, too. Adolescence is a difficult and painful time even under the best of circumstances. Kids' hormones are in an uproar. They feel uncomfortable in their bodies. They want to be adult but in many ways they are still children. They act tough but are incredibly vulnerable. The pain of their first loves goes right to the core, and even though as adults we know they will make many choices in relationships before they make a definitive life decision, it is a mistake to minimize a first love's

meaning. Much drug overdose and other adolescent suicide, particularly among males, is the result of rejection. Your availability to listen and discuss without judging or showing the "right" way will reduce pain. Essentially, this principle could be summarized as a suggestion to "keep the lines of communication open."

If the lines of communication are open, you may help steer off a problem before it starts, and the chances increase that if your child does get into trouble, he will come to you.

If you suspect your child has a problem:

1. Know what adolescent treatment centers are available to you. There is treatment available regardless of your financial situation. Find out how to set your child up for treatment.
2. Join a Parents' Anonymous group or a tough-love group. This will connect you to people in situations similar to yours, whom you can call when you can't take the pressure, and will help you to learn effective strategies for regaining control in your own home. Groups like these help you learn how to behave so you can't be manipulated.
3. Have your child assessed for alcohol and/or drug addiction. Skilled professionals can see through her bravado.

There have been many circumstances in which alarmed parents have called our Institute for Counseling and Training, in West Caldwell, New Jersey, where we specialize in working with dysfunctional families and individuals. We have met with them, met with their child, and if we shared the parents' concern, made arrangements with an appropriate treatment center and had the child in treatment before he knew what hit him.

Arrangements can also be made with schools so that no time is lost in the academic program.

There will be resistance at first. This is predictable, but the inevitable outcome is gratitude. After all, you have literally saved your child's life. You cannot be an effective parent to an abusing adolescent and be popular. Actually, you can't be an effective parent to any adolescent and be popular. It just doesn't go with the role. Setting and enforcing reasonable limits is to everyone's benefit, regardless of the child's reaction.

I don't know any parents who are not very concerned that their children will abuse alcohol and/or drugs. There is no way to be complacent about this one, and frankly, I think anyone who is complacent about it is foolish. Too many kids whom one "would never have thought," have gotten trapped. There are no easy answers and anyone who writes a book that says do this and that and your kids will not do drugs does not do you a service. There are, however, some things to keep in mind.

If you grew up in a family where there was an addiction, chances are you either developed an addiction of your own or have an aversion to alcohol and/or drugs. Nevertheless, because your children have your body chemistry they stand a greater chance than other kids of becoming addicted. That's just the way it is. You need to watch for some of these signs very early and you need to inform your pediatrician of your family history. If your pediatrician does not find the information useful, you probably need to question him or her further to be sure he or she will serve you well.

It is not unusual for children of alcoholics to have paradoxical responses to medication. A medication designed to have a sedative effect may agitate them. Also, these children very often require a larger dosage than the one usually appropriate to their size and weight. It is not at all unusual for alcoholics to have blood sugar–related problems, so you need to be watchful of your child's sugar intake and related mood swings. At our institute we also see a disproportionate number of children who have perceptual problems and other neurological problems.

This information is not based on medical research but on observation over the years, and doctors with whom I work tend to agree that one need be mindful of these tendencies within this population.

One of the implications of this is that good nutrition is very important to keeping your child's system in balance. You may be an expert in nutrition, in which case you may skip this next section, but otherwise it has been my experience that many folks who grew up in troubled families don't know the first thing about how to plan a balanced diet for either themselves or their children.

I remember in particular a client whom I worked with at overcoming an eating disorder. One day I just happened to say, "If you did not have this eating disorder, how would you eat?"

She looked at me quizzically.

"Frankly," she said, "I have no idea. When I was growing up you just grabbed what you could!"

Others have said, "In our family, food was the remedy for everything. If you were happy you ate, if you were sad you ate, if you were frustrated you ate, if you were anxious you ate. It's not as if you even sat at the table. You just grabbed. So it would either be something you could put between two pieces of bread, or sugar. I thought everyone ate like that."

And others still have said, "In our house we all sat down to dinner together and that would be the signal for my parents to start a fight. My stomach would automatically tense up and I'd feel nauseous. We weren't allowed to leave the table until our plates were clean, and I'd just wolf down my food so I could flee."

I'm certain there is much you yourself could add to this discussion. The point is that you need to find out what is appropriate nutrition for your children and yourself. If your child's diet is balanced she will be less likely to crave sweets and sodas and the like. This does not mean that as soon as they can they won't go after the stuff you put off limits, but it does cut down somewhat on their consumption of it and at the very least they are learning good habits.

Much of the craving for alcohol is the craving for carbohydrate. If you ever observe recovering alcoholics you see that it is not unusual for them to eat large quantities of ice cream, cookies, and other sugars.

It is important that your children know about their risks of developing the disease of alcoholism whether they want to hear it or not. Children of alcoholics resent the fact that they run a higher risk of becoming alcoholic than many of their friends do. I don't blame them. I would resent it, too, if I were in their place. However, their resentment doesn't change the facts nor does it lessen your responsibility to give them the information.

If you developed an addiction when you were growing up, one of the main reasons you did was that you needed to numb out. Your family situation may have been too painful for you to bear and so you turned to substances as a way not to feel.

Now that you have children of your own, ask yourself honestly whether or not you are providing them with an environment that makes them want to come home and that makes them feel safe when they get there. Are you welcoming to your children? Do they feel special in your presence? Do their friends want to come to your house? Is your home a place where you want to be? Do you feel welcome and safe? Do not minimize the stress that children experience in their daily lives. School is a stressful place. School exerts pressure to conform, pressure to perform, pressure to be accepted.

It's not easy being a kid. When your kids come home from school, is some of that pressure relieved, or must they continue to fight for approval and to ward off danger? Many young people on the other side of a drug problem have said to me, "Jan, don't tell me I was a dope to use dope. It was the only friend I had. It was the only way to make the pain go away."

I agree with them. But I point out that their only friend quickly becomes their worst enemy. At first you take the drugs and in relatively short order the drugs take you.

It is up to the parents to provide a safe harbor for their children and to do everything they can to make sure this doesn't happen.

If you didn't have a safe harbor of this sort to go to when you were growing up, ask yourself what you are offering your children now. If your partner is not invested in creating a healthy climate for your children, do not fool yourself into believing you can do it alone. You can do your best, but if someone else is creating a stressful home environment, you can neither protect yourself nor your children from it. If this is the case in your home, I recommend that you and your children both join support groups to learn the principles of detachment. This will help, but it will only help by reducing the downside. This approach does not offer an up side. I do not say this to discourage you, but only to let you know the truth of what you are up against. If you are in this situation, it is a difficult situation and it cannot be minimized.

It is very difficult to be realistic about children and drugs and alcohol when the stakes are so high. It is not unusual to either minimize or to overreact. I myself have been known to wonder out loud why the neighbors would put beer cans in my garbage cans. And I also admit that I threw out a sterile respirator my son needed for his lifeguard job because I decided it was a bong. The father of a young woman I know was so afraid of what she might be doing that he actually took her bedroom door off its hinges.

Kids love to talk about how their parents "freak out." They find it funny. Parents don't find it quite so amusing. But unlike the kids, they know there is no such thing as immortality. Parents are adults. They are realistic. And they have realistic fears.

Adolescents experiment. It is in their nature. They see themselves as immortal, they are impulsive, and there is very little they won't test out. Kids see their parents as fools and kids believe they can do whatever they want without losing control. If your children don't overtly seem to fit this description, they may just be better at hiding it than most.

Adolescence creates a natural friction between parent and child, and drugs are an area where this stress point gets played out.

All you can do is everything you can do. You never know when you will be heard or what action of yours will make a difference.

And there is the chance that you will make a difference.

Joanne told me this anecdote about her son's first semester

at college. Bart made it very clear that while the other kids were getting drunk and throwing up all the time, he was not. She was pleased, and curious to know why this was so.

"The truth is, Mom," he said, "I think I do it to spite you. The very first time I had too much to drink, I remember sticking my head in the toilet and retching my guts out. You heard me, came into the bathroom, and very gently put your hand on my head. You said, 'There, there, dear. It could have been worse. You might not have gotten sick.' Then you walked out leaving me to my vomit. Somehow you got a big kick out of the whole thing, and right then and there I vowed, 'Never Again!' "

N I N E

STAGES OF CHILD
DEVELOPMENT

a) In a healthy family demands made on children are age-
and developmentally appropriate.

b) In an unhealthy family the child is asked to demonstrate
pseudomaturity or is infantilized.

BONNIE REPORTS, "My mother left me with a two-month-old
baby to care for when I was eight while she and my stepfather
went into the bar below our apartment to drink. When the baby
got "too fussy" I was supposed to stamp my feet on the floor to
signal her to come up. One night there was too much noise in
the bar and she didn't hear me. I was so overwhelmed I just cried
right along with the baby."

Gloria identifies. "It was my job to take care of my little sister
and I hated it and I hated her. I had to drag her with me
everywhere I went. She was always in the way. When I combed

her hair, I would pull at the tangles until she cried, and I loved doing it. And to this day we don't have a relationship. I resent her and she resents me. I know my mother had to work and we didn't have any money for babysitters, but I still resent it. She never even thanked me for what I did for her. She'd just yell at me if the house wasn't clean or if I forgot to do the wash. Damn it! I was a mother at eight years old while all the other kids were out playing.

"I don't ask my own kids to do anything. I think there's something wrong with that too. I don't want them to grow up the way I did, but it's hard to know what is fair to ask of them and what isn't. Whenever I ask them to do anything they complain, and I end up feeling guilty and backing down. I'm such a wimp. But I think mostly I'm confused."

Kevin was born with a heart problem. As the result of the stress and restrictions the disease placed on the family, neither Kevin's mother or father wanted their son out of their sight. To each other, they rationalized their behavior by saying they felt all their attention was required to keep Kevin healthy, and that having to worry about where their son was would not be in his best interest. As a result, Kevin was not even allowed to sleep over at a friend's house.

The truth was that it was difficult for them to admit Kevin was getting older. The problem he had had as a baby had been corrected. Soon he would be growing away from them, and as he discovered his own talents and tasks as an individual in his own right, he might not be as available to them. If he became independent, he would be more difficult to control, and control had been very important to them within the demanding health situation. Just as importantly, because Kevin's parents had a poor self-image of their ability to nurture, they were also afraid Kevin might like someone else's family better than his own and they would be shown lacking.

As an adult, Kevin was able to realize he had been infantilized by his parents. He found out when he entered therapy after beginning to wonder why it was that he was so terrified about the idea of having children of his own.

Letting go of a child is always difficult, and it is even more difficult when the child has a special need. But it has to be done.

Sometimes, the same child is made to fill the shoes of both a pseudomature child and an infantilized child at the parent's whim. The child of a mother who is alcoholic could end up cleaning up her mother's vomit, or cooking for the family or putting her mother to bed. But between episodes, when she is feeling remorseful, the same mother could take over everything for the child out of her own guilt and forbid the child from doing anything for herself. This child doesn't go through the usual developmental stages, either. As an adult with children of her own, she too will review her past and ask, "What is enough? What is too much?"

You may also need to look at some aspects of your childhood through a new lens. Context often determines how we view a particular behavior, such as doing chores or helping to take care of younger siblings. If we were unhappy about the circumstances surrounding the behavior, the skills involved can get dismissed as well. And sometimes dismissing them can be a mistake.

An example I have used many times involves a young man I know who is a member of a functional family. When he was five years old, this young man would come home from school and prepare himself a tuna fish sandwich. By himself, he would open the can of tuna fish, mix it with mayonnaise, toast himself some bread, and put it all together. Anyone who saw him do this thought it was adorable and that this was part of a conscious plan to teach the child independence. The young man was praised for his behavior, and gained quite a bit of confidence from it.

If you grew up in a dysfunctional family, chances are that you too could make a sandwich at that age. You were probably also taking care of your other siblings as well. Your skill was the same, but the response to you was different. For you, the same behavior that earned praise and confidence for the child of a functional family would have attracted pity. Others would have felt sorry for you. "That poor child is taking on adult roles prematurely," people would have said.

As a result you would feel sorry for yourself and protective of your family. You also felt angry and stuck.

Context is critical. For some of you, the question will not be one of skills learned but rather one of attitudes. The same behavior. But add a different context and a different response, and the result is a different self-image.

Children are born dependent and spend much of their lives trying to individuate. The job of the parent is to assist in this process. Assisting in the process means finding the delicate balance between dependence and independence every step of the way. Children will constantly fight for the right to have or do it "their way" and you need to know when to allow them this right and when to say no.

Sometimes the lines are clear. No, the two-year-old *cannot cross the street* without holding on to your hand, regardless of how strongly he feels about it. But other decisions are not as clear, such as, "Can I watch another half hour of television before I do my homework?"

If you grew up in a dysfunctional family, careful consideration was not given to these kinds of decisions. You either did whatever you felt like or you were restricted without any reason understood by you. You may have been given responsibilities way beyond those appropriate for your age or even way beyond those appropriate for a child altogether, or you may have been infantilized and not allowed to do anything.

Needless to say, this makes the job of encouraging your child to do what is age-appropriate and what is appropriate for him as an individual all the more difficult for you because you have no models and no data bank for this skill. And to top it all off, doing so is difficult for all parents. Our own temperament also comes into play as we try to help a child individuate. One person will let a small child make his own peanut butter and jelly sandwich and pour his own milk even if it means there will be a mess to clean up afterward. Other parents would not be able to deal with the mess and so they will choose to make the sandwich for the child. Still other parents will compromise and just make sure to cover the surfaces and then let the child do her thing. I mention this to stress that in addition to your assessment of whether or not the activity in question is developmentally appropriate, there are many other things that come into play when you make decisions about what level of independence to allow your children.

Because as a result of your own history you also may be unsure about what a child is capable of at each developmental stage, here are some guidelines you can follow. The process of helping a child to individuate is not all guesswork. These guidelines will also explain to you how you positively influence your child's future when her developmental needs are met appropriately. They will also show you how each stage presents challenges and inconveniences for you the parent that are okay for you to feel unhappy about or resentful of, or that are okay for your kids to feel unhappy about or resentful of, depending on the particular skill or behavior in question. They'll also show you what's not okay.

Our awareness of creating a healthy climate for children to develop in must begin before birth. Bear in mind that good prenatal care will increase the chances of having a healthy baby. Injunctions against smoking and drinking are not to be taken lightly. If this poses a problem for you, seek help. The stakes involved are very high ones.

THE PRENATAL PERIOD

The prenatal period is a time in which a couple can begin to share responsibility in planning for the child. If you decide on natural childbirth, now is the time to take the classes together so the father can have the opportunity to assist at the birth.

You can make joint decisions about furniture for the baby, and about how he or she will fit into your lives.

An attitude of shared parenting responsibility begins at this age. And ideally, it continues throughout the child's life—both parents will need to share in the 3:00 A.M. feeding and in walking the floors when the baby is upset. Even if the mother is nursing, a bottle can be prepared so she can have relief and her partner can participate.

Birth to Eighteen Months

The period from birth to eighteen months is the period in which a child develops a sense of trust or mistrust in the world around him. If the child's needs are met appropriately by the parents, the child will develop a sense of trust. If the needs are not met, he will develop mistrust. The psychologist Erik Erikson describes this period as the first of five psychosocial developmental stages, and as a building block for subsequent stages.

The following are the eventual behavioral outcomes of meeting a child's needs at this stage and of not meeting a child's needs at this stage:

People who have a highly developed sense of trust are able to ask for help or emotional support; believe others will come through for them; believe people are generally good, and see others in a positive light; are open and disclosing around others; receive compliments and gifts easily but like to give as well, and have no difficulty sharing things.

People with an undeveloped sense of trust react in the opposite way. They have trouble asking for help or emotional support; don't believe that others will come through for them; believe people are generally bad or evil and see others in a negative light; are guarded and closed around others; find it difficult to receive gifts and compliments and would much prefer to be the giver, and have problems sharing things with others.

While the child is developing a sense of trust, the child's parents are finding out that infancy is not only a time of great joy but also one of great exhaustion.

When you see the first real smile or hear the first giggles, these things will thrill you. You will, however, also find yourself tired all the time because babies need to be fed around the clock. One of your greatest joys will occur when your baby finally sleeps through the night. You will learn to nap when the baby sleeps— hardly what you bargained for. Sometimes you will feel annoyed and frustrated with your baby.

These are normal feelings. There is nothing wrong with these feelings.

As a result, when you are the parent of an infant, it is not your fault if you resent the fact that:

1. Your infant needs to eat every four hours around the clock regardless of how tired you are.
2. Your infant finds ways to leak through leak-proof diapers and onto your good clothes.
3. You do not automatically fall in love with your infant. Loving a baby is learned behavior. It is different than loving the idea of having a baby.
4. Your baby is colicky. Colic has to do with the development of your baby's nervous system or gastrointestinal system. Colic does not develop because you are a lousy, nervous, or ineffective parent.

In summary, there is nothing wrong in having these feelings or experiences; they are normal for parents of babies at this developmental stage. However, there is something wrong if you:

1. Don't keep your baby warm and dry and fed.
2. Don't comfort and hold her when she's distressed, because you "can't stand it another minute."

Not doing these things can create mistrust and impact on the baby's future developmental stages.

Eighteen Months to Three Years

Eighteen months to three years is the period in which the child develops a sense of autonomy if her developmental needs are met, or a sense of shame and doubt if they are not met. If you have learned that the world is safe and trustworthy from birth to eighteen months, then you can begin to test it out without fear. This period is the second psychosocial stage, another building block for future stages.

People who have a highly developed sense of autonomy like to make their own decisions; are able to say no to requests made of them without feeling guilty; can express themselves in terms of what they will or what they want to do; resist being controlled by others; can work well alone or with others; can finish what they start; can work in either structured or unstructured situations; can follow their inner voice; are at ease in a group; and maintain a sense of order and organization in their lives.

People who have a highly developed sense of shame and doubt prefer that decisions be made for them; have difficulty saying no; express themselves in terms of "shoulds"; allow themselves to be dominated; prefer not to work alone; tend to procrastinate; need structure and direction; are outer- rather than inner-directed; are uneasy and self-conscious in social situations; and tend to want things "just so" in order to avoid criticism.

When you are the parent of a toddler, you will find your child is very enchanting and very frustrating at the same time. A toddler's first steps and first words are a delight to even the most sophisticated parent. But the child is also in the stage of pre-rational thought, so you will find you are repeating yourself over and over and you will find you are unable to responsibly take your eyes off your child even for a second—because as a result of being in the stage of prerational thought, your toddler is constantly doing things that are not safe.

As a result, when you have a toddler it is important to know that it is not your fault if you resent the fact that:

1. Your toddler puts everything into his mouth.
2. Your toddler is a mess as soon as he is dressed.
3. Your toddler knocks over everything.
4. Your toddler throws a tantrum if he doesn't get his way.
5. Your toddler keeps running off but screams if you are out of his sight.
6. All the other kids are toilet trained and yours holds on.
7. Your toddler says no to everything.

These behaviors are part of the developmental stage your child is passing through, and although they help develop autonomy in the toddler they can be very frustrating to an adult. However, it *is* your fault if:

1. Your toddler can reach cleaning fluids or medicines.
2. You don't have a change of clothing available or if you can't tolerate mess.
3. There are valuable things around for your toddler to break.
4. You lose your temper and punish your toddler in an abusive way.
5. You don't walk out on and ignore a temper tantrum.
6. You get angry at your toddler because he's still in diapers.
7. You get angry when your toddler says no, instead of giving him real choices about other toys to play with or different foods to eat.

Doing these things can foster shame and doubt in your toddler.

THREE TO SIX YEARS

Three to six years is the stage in which the child will develop initiative (a natural outgrowth of the autonomy developed during the toddler years) or will become driven by guilt (which can be the result of having developed feelings of shame and doubt in the toddler years). Erikson describes this as the third psychosocial stage, yet another building block for future stages.

In adulthood, those with a developed sense of initiative prefer to get on with what needs to be done to complete the task at hand; like accepting new challenges; tend to be self-starters; tend to be effective leaders; tend to set goals and then set out to accomplish them; tend to have high energy levels; have a strong sense of personal adequacy; and seem to enjoy "making things happen."

In adulthood, those who have developed a sense of guilt are inclined to resist new challenges; are not real self-starters; tend to be ineffective leaders; may set goals but have problems getting them accomplished; tend to have low energy levels; have a weak sense of personal adequacy; prefer not to stir things up; and tend to focus moralistically on those things in life that are "wrong."

The child at this age is more civilized and reasonable than he was as a toddler. He is fun to be with and can understand and participate in activities. At this stage, children also feel their oats and test limits as they begin to individuate. As a result, when you are the parent of a preschooler, it is *not* your fault if:

1. Your child does not want to share.
2. Your child regresses sometimes and behaves as if she were two, and either acts out or withdraws.
3. Your child is incredibly demanding and constantly tests limits.
4. Your child says "I hate you" and is defiant.
5. Your child can't sit still and gets wild or loud.

All of these types of behavior are part of developing initiative. You did nothing wrong if your preschooler behaves this way. You are more likely to have a problem if your child *doesn't* behave this way. However, it *is* your fault if:

1. You force your preschooler to share rather than put that toy away and find another toy he is willing to share.
2. You cannot accept the fact that a new growth spurt or a new

event such as the birth of a baby will cause regression in the child which he cannot explain.

3. You don't set limits: e.g., "You cannot do that. I do not allow anyone to hit me."

4. You don't recognize that your child's behavior is developmental and the only way he knows how to separate and individuate, and as a result you take it personallly.

5. You don't avoid confrontation by removing the child from your space. (A "time-out" chair may cool things down.)

If you behave this way you can develop guilt in your child.

SIX TO TWELVE YEARS

The period from six to twelve years old marks the stage in which a child either develops a sense of industry (in part based on the successful outcome of the previous stages, which gives the child a sense of being internally motivated) or a sense of inferiority (in part based on an outcome of the previous stages in which the child has gained a sense of being externally motivated, by shame, doubt, guilt, etc.). Known as "school age," this time period is described by Erikson as the fourth psychosocial stage and building block for future stages.

People who have a sense of industry enjoy learning about new things and ideas; reflect a healthy balance between doing what they have to do and what they like to do; are curious about how and why things work the way they do; enjoy experimenting with new combinations and new ideas and arriving at new syntheses; are excited by the idea of being producers; like the recognition that producing things brings (which reinforces their sense of industry); develop the habit of completing their work through steady attention and persevering diligence; have a sense of pride in doing at least one thing well; take criticism well and use it to improve their performance; and tend to be persistent.

People who have a sense of inferiority do not particularly

enjoy learning about new things and ideas; tend to concentrate mostly on what they believe they have to do and neglect what they would like to do; are not terribly curious about why and how things work; prefer staying with what is known; are not attracted so much by new ways as by proven ways; tend to feel threatened and even guilty about the idea of being producers; would like the recognition that production brings but find a sense of inferiority gets in the way of producing; develop a habit of procrastinating about their work; have problems taking pride in their work, believing it is worth the trouble; take criticism poorly and use it as a reason to stop trying; and tend to have a weak sense of persistence.

School age is mostly a very nice age. Children of this age are much more civilized than younger children, and can take care of their own physical needs. On the other hand, this age also has its challenges and problems. The school-age child's world expands to the point that the child develops important relationships outside the family, particularly tight friends of the same sex. The family is no longer the child's whole world. The relationship with friends becomes much more important. The child may be antagonistic toward the opposite sex, and want to be with his same-sex friends all the time.

As a result, some parents become concerned that their children may be homosexual, and the truth is that they do check out each other's body parts. But this is part of normal development, and does not necessarily indicate a sex-partner preference, but rather a stage in the development of a sexual identity.

Children of this age also become collectors, and they collect anything from stamps, cards, and coins to bugs. They also develop rituals, and certainly would never ever "step on a crack 'cause it'll break your mother's back."

Along with the child's greater independence comes a whole new set of needs. One of the most difficult needs for the parent to fulfill is car-pooling. These are the years of lessons and religious school and parties, and also of friends who don't live on the block. These are also the years of having dinner one place and sleeping another and fighting over whether or not it is necessary to practice the piano.

As a result, parents of school-age children discover they are spending lots of time in stop-and-go traffic.

These are also the years when you give your kids the advantages you didn't have, or which you did have but didn't use to good benefit. This is the stage in which your kids will beg for a pet and swear on all that is precious to them that the pet will not become your problem: they will feed it and walk it and keep it clean and all that other good stuff.

Forget it. What they will do is love it, and it is important that you don't get sucked into their magical thinking. Of course the pet will become your problem. But loving a pet and being loved back by the pet can be an important experience for children to have. The unconditional love a pet offers a person is very special. Many of you, in reflecting back on your own childhoods, know what that love meant to you.

As a result, if you are the parent of a school-age child it is *not* your fault if:

1. You feel used when you have to drive your kids everywhere. Yes, you are put upon, but your children have few other options. Your kids need your assistance to make their world work. After all, they can go just so far on their bikes, and bikes are no good in the snow or in the dark.
2. You need time to get used to all the sleepovers and parties and you find you are becoming very sensitive to the difference between supervision and intrusion.

Children need to participate in these activities in order to develop a sense of industry, and require your participation to do so. However, it *is* your fault if:

1. Your child cannot participate in activities or see her friends because you will not provide transportation for her or make arrangements for her.

2. You intrude on your child's friendships and social relationships, or discourage your child from having them because it is inconvenient for you or because you need your child to perform adult functions in the household or want to discourage your child's independence.

Children denied these experiences at this age can end up with a sense of inferiority.

It is up to you. It may be that in your childhood you didn't have a parent available to you to fulfill these needs for you, either because you were needed at home or because getting around was your problem. It is true your children are more fortunate, but they appear to feel entitled and certainly not grateful.

Frankly, there is no reason for them to be grateful. They're just kids. But it's true that an occasional "thank you" wouldn't hurt.

TWELVE TO TWENTY YEARS

These years, known as the teenage years, are those in which children struggle with identity issues and in which the process of developing into either an inner- or outer-directed individual culminates.

People who have a strong sense of identity have a stable self-concept that is not easily changed; are able to combine short-term goals with long-range plans; are less susceptible to the shifting whims of peer-pressure influences; tend to have reasonably high levels of self-acceptance; are able to make decisions without undue wavering and indecisiveness; tend to be optimistic about themselves, others, and life in general; tend to believe they are responsible for what happens to them whether what happens to them is good or bad; are able to seek self-acceptance directly by being their own person; are able to be physically and emotionally close to another person without fearing a loss of self; tend to be open-minded; and have a sense of self that is not dependent on being "right."

People who have identity confusion tend to have an unstable self-concept marked by ups and downs; tend to set short-term goals, but have trouble establishing long-range plans; are more susceptible to the shifting whims of peer-pressure influences; tend to have rather low levels of self-acceptance; are apt to have trouble making decisions because they fear they will make the wrong ones; tend to have a somewhat cynical attitude about themselves, others, and life in general; tend to believe that what happens to them is largely out of their hands—a matter of "fate" or "breaks"; are inclined to seek self-acceptance indirectly by being what they believe others want them to be; are inclined to have trouble being physically and emotionally close to another person without being either too dependent on or too separate from that person; tend to be cognitively inflexible; and possess a sense of self that resides heavily on being "right."*

Teenagers have one clear and present enemy: themselves.

Children in this age group seem driven to self-destruct, and despite their relative life experience when compared to children in other groups, need your protection and intervention at this stage as much as they do at any other.

The best advice I can give you as you pull your hair out is to try to hang on to the following thought: "It's not really me she's out to get, it's herself."

That perspective may help you to get through this exciting period in your child's life. Remember that you cannot be both popular and effective with your teenager and that maintaining order is your job.

If you are the parent of a teenager, it is *not* your fault if:

1. You and your teenager are constantly at war.
2. Your teenager treats you as if you don't know anything.
3. Your teenager fights limits tooth and nail.

---

*These lists of characteristics have been developed from tables with the permission of Dr. Don E. Hamachek, from his article "Evaluating Self-Concept and Ego Development Within Erikson's Psychosocial Framework." *Journal of Counseling and Development,"* vol. 66 (1988), pp. 354–360.

4. You are embarrassed about the way you feel about your own child.
5. Your teenager believes she is invincible and ignores your pleadings concerning safety.
6. You feel like a dismal failure as a parent.

These feelings are natural ones to have as your teenager pulls out all the stops and pushes all the limits in her tireless yet developmentally appropriate campaign to establish her identity. However, it *is* your fault if:

1. You allow your teenager to win the war.
2. You ignore it if your teenager is disrespectful.
3. You don't enforce reasonable limits no matter what it takes.
4. You don't let your teenager know what you really think.
5. You have not made clear the risks involved in unsafe driving, drinking, or sex.
6. You give up because you feel overwhelmed or decide further persistence would be a threat to your sobriety.

These behaviors could result in your child's identity confusion—or death.

In summary, different stages of child development require different parental responses. Fortunately, as children progress and develop and mature, so do you as parents. Kids do what comes naturally, and if you go with the flow, in most cases the same will be true for you as well.

Many people are amused when children dress up and imitate adults, and are similarly amused when an adult puts on a diaper on New Year's Eve. In both cases, the humor lies in the discordancy. Unfortunately, for many of us these behaviors hold no humor at all because we have lived through them.

Don't feel bad if you didn't know the things discussed above. Your parents didn't raise you in a developmentally appropriate way, so you couldn't have known them. But now you have gained the awareness you need to raise your own children in the developmentally appropriate way you were denied. There are scores and scores of books available on the subject of child development where you can read more about this if you want to.

Fortunately, the confusion can stop here.

T E N

LIVING WITH LOVE

a) In a healthy family children are affirmed regularly and automatically.

b) In an unhealthy family children are made to feel unworthy and unlovable.

"How could you be so stupid?"
"If you can't say anything nice, don't say anything at all."
"When are you going to grow up?"
"Stop crying or I'll give you something to cry about."
"I hope you have a kid just like yourself someday."
"Quit acting so childish."
"You ruin everything you touch."
"Shape up or ship out."
"You'll be the death of me."
"What did you do *this* time?"
"How can I love you if you do that?"

Children crave attention. They do not care about the nature of the attention. If they get negative attention, that is preferable to getting no attention at all. It is confusing to grow up in this way. If you do, as an adult you will believe those who are angry at you are demonstrating that they care about you, and you will regard with suspicion all those who affirm you.

The messages of your childhood become a part of the way you see yourself. If those messages were negative, you will not have good feelings about yourself or about the world around you. This history cannot help but influence you as a parent, so it is important to explore your own parental messages fully.

In the mid 1970s a Dr. Tom Harris wrote a book called *I'm Okay, You're Okay*. This book was an immediate best-seller and deservedly so. It explained the notion of transactional analysis in a way that the nonprofessional could understand and use. The concepts Dr. Harris discussed are useful in understanding why you struggle the way you do with being the kind of parent you so much want to be.

Dr. Harris wrote about the idea that within each of us there resides a child part. This is the part of us that feels, that has the "aha of new experiences," the part of us that is curious. The child part is the place in us where we are free and unencumbered and available to life and all it has in store. This part has no limits and no boundaries. When we are in our child part we are truly free.

The parent in us is the place where the rules are: *You can do this. You don't do that. You should believe this. You shouldn't believe that.* The parent in us provides a road map for our moral and ethical system. It is the emotional response to the child part.

The adult in us processes what it learns from the child part and the parent part and decides rationally how to behave.

We then internalize all three parts. That is the way we live our lives. For instance:

1. The child in us wants to run across the street.
2. The parent in us warns us to be careful.
3. The adult then looks both ways before running across the street.

This is a rather simple concept to grasp if you grew up in a healthy family. But if you did not, you may be passing along injunctions to your children that misrepresent you and represent the dysfunctional background you come from instead. Chances are that if parental responses to you were negative, your family was dysfunctional. Dysfunctional responses to you would include such messages as:

"You're stupid."
"You can't do anything right."
"You'll never amount to anything."
"I really wanted a boy."

If, for example, the child within you has a new idea and the parent within you reminds you that you are stupid because that is what one or both of your parents told you whenever you had a new idea, the adult in you will most likely keep the idea to himself.

However, all is not lost. The first step to take is to become aware of what is going on inside you. What are the negative parental injunctions that still influence you? Make a list like the one above and the one that begins this chapter. Then list specific examples of how you behaved or still behave as a result of each negative parental injunction on your list.

Next change the negative injunctions of your childhood to affirmations. Change each critical parental statement to a message of support. Reverse the judgments. For example:

NEGATIVE	POSITIVE
"When are you going to grow up?"	"I'm just fine just the way I am."
"I really wanted a boy."	"I'm lovable."
"You'll never amount to anything."	"I'm worthwhile."
"Stop crying or I'll give you something to cry about."	"Whatever I feel is okay."

Give specific examples of how you would have behaved differently if you'd had the new message. Are there ways in which your parenting is influenced by the messages you carry inside? The answer is yes. The answers don't have to be profound. Very simple answers will do.

When Don tried this exercise, he found that one of the things he had learned from the parental injunctions he had received in his childhood was that he was "different" than others.

"I carry that with me to this day," Don said, "and I rarely shake the feeling. When I was growing up, all my friends had bicycles with thin tires while my bike had balloon tires because 'it was safer.' And while all my friends wore sneakers to school, I wasn't allowed to because 'my arches would fall.' I didn't really care if those lousy tires were safer, and I didn't understand and didn't care what a fallen arch was. All I knew was that I was different from the other kids, and that this made me feel inferior to them.

"As a result, I go to the other extreme with my own children. I'll buy them the exact bicycle that 'everyone's riding,' or the exact designer sneaker that 'everyone's wearing,' and they make the final choice about what they want themselves. If fitting in is as important to them as it was to me, I will champion their right to do so."

The fact that you are now an adult and have a child or children of your own does not mean the negative injunctions you received from your parents will stop undermining you. It is important to realize this because these injunctions will make you feel insecure, and you were probably insecure to begin with. Every new parent is.

The message Sharon received from her mother was a simple one: "My way is the only way." This message was non-negotiable. Since she had grown up with it, it was not surprising that Sharon felt conflicted every time she chose a way different from her mother's. It was also impossible for Sharon not to second-guess everything she did, with her mother's approval or lack of it in mind, so she would often feel herself on shaky ground.

Sharon attended one of my groups, and she rarely said a word. Even if she did speak, she always prefaced her contributions with something like "I don't know if this makes any sense," or "I hope this doesn't sound stupid."

The others would tell her that her thoughts had great value, but that support did not influence Sharon's inner voice to the contrary.

That is because negative parental messages have to do with you and your relationship with yourself and not with your relationship with other people. Why can't I let myself go and have a good time, you may ask. You were told you weren't worth it and unconsciously you live it out.

Hugh is another member of the same group. Hugh is able to take care of everyone's needs but his own. He will be sure everyone at the party has a drink and someone to talk to, and that the ashtrays are clean, and only later will he complain, "I really wanted an opportunity to get to know Sue better and we scarcely said a word to each other all night."

Until someone points out to Hugh that he only considers himself in retrospect, he is unaware of the part he plays in creating his own problem.

Do behaviors like these affect your children? Of course. They have to, even if you don't want them to. Children learn by what they see. If, for instance, you keep your thoughts and feelings to yourself like Sharon does, your children will learn this is the way to be. If you always put others first the way Hugh does, they will learn that lesson as well.

Although Sharon is unsure about some things, she does have very conscious beliefs about raising children. Sharon believes children should be allowed to do, to explore, to try out within the limits of safety. She believes children should be given enough leeway to be able to feel mastery over their environment, but not enough leeway that they become overly frustrated as a result. As a result, her children are willing to test out new things and stretch their worlds.

When Sharon's kids were little and wanted to dress themselves, she would encourage them. If this meant the day started
a little later then it would have otherwise or that a sock went
on inside out, that was of no consequence. What was of consequence was that the children had accomplished something they
felt proud of, and that Sharon could feel their delight.

One day Sharon's mother came to visit.

Sharon's three-year-old promptly announced, "Look,
Grandma, I dressed all by myself!"

Sharon's mother turned to her and said, "With you for a
mother, what choice is there?"

Sharon's mother's way had been to dress the child so
that everything was perfectly coordinated, and as far as her
mother was concerned, that was the only way. Sharon felt proud
of herself that she had overcome the programming of her childhood, but she still felt lousy that she wanted her mother's approval.

What messages are you sending along to your children? If you
don't want to pass your injunctions along, you must consciously
and conscientiously alter the messages you send. Remember that
the parent is the guide and the teacher. So changing the injunction does not mean you should not send any injunction.
What it does mean is that you should send a positive message
instead.

For example, Sharon's mother's parental injunction, "My way
is the only way," needs to be changed to:

"Sometimes my way is the best way, but your way is worth
hearing about and sometimes that way will work, too."

This means that *no*, you cannot run into the street, but yes,
you can have peanut butter and jelly instead of tuna fish if you
prefer.

Same behavior, different response, different self-feeling.

Think of the skills you learned as a child. Are you glad you
were able to do the things you knew how to do regardless of the
reasons you could do them? It may be that even as a very young

child you had to take care of younger brothers and sisters. This was unfortunate because it interfered with your own childhood. It is all the more unfortunate that you did not get strokes but instead were constantly criticized: "Didn't you see he had a rip in his pants?"

However, it is impressive to know you can be careful with another life, that you were able to do things like prepare food, help someone else get dressed, and all the other things that are involved with raising young children. You may even have done the wash and the cooking in your family at a very early age. It is unfortunate this was your job. But impressive that you had the capability.

Having older siblings take care of younger really sets up such resentment on the part of all the siblings—in the elder for having to take care of another sibling and in the younger for having to be taken care of and "bossed by" the other—that many of these relationships never heal. The siblings are in effect set up for lifelong resentment. A patient of mine once said, "When I was little, I used to wash the dirt off of my little sister's face and I made sure that it hurt like hell."

Siblings don't like to be forced to take care of each other this way. And forcing them to do this is destructive for all concerned. But this isn't to say that it's never appropriate for an older child to babysit a younger child—members of a family help each other out. That's part of being a family.

You may have learned other skills in a negative way that are constructive, too. For example, as a child you may have heard the injunction "You ruin everything you touch," and as a result you became very careful with objects. However, in a healthy family you would also have learned to be careful with objects simply because you learned how to respect other people's boundaries and possessions.

Some of the skills you learned as the result of a negative injunction are skills you will want your child to possess, and some you won't. Then teach them those things that are valuable and age-appropriate. Children want to participate in the household and it is healthy to help them be part of the process. And sometimes it's fun for kids to be in charge. It is only when the parent is replaced by the child in terms of household responsibility that behavior becomes destructive.

So what to do when you need help? One solution is to pay your child to do something you would otherwise pay someone else to do if you didn't have access to your responsible child. Babysitting is a good example of a need that can be handled in this way. Whether or not you pay the going rate is up to you. If money is not very available in your household, you could reward the child in some other way, such as letting him stay up later, instead.

When you were growing up, you may have felt more like a used and abused object than a valued and appreciated family member. The idea that children have rights was not in your experience.

In some rural economies children were bred for a purpose. People wanted to have as many children as possible in order to have as many hands as possible to work on the farm. This book does not support this notion. This is not the reason for having children in our society or at this time. Rather, the purpose for having a child is to create an individual who has a fully developed self and who feels good about being him- or herself. This is done by providing an environment which best serves this process, an environment in which the child instinctively knows, "I exist for me—I don't exist for you." Statements like "You can't do this to me" contradict this basic right. "I don't like what you're doing" is a far better representation of your feelings and the child's rights.

In looking at yourself as a parent, it is important to recognize that children have rights and to offer them to your children. If you are unclear about what all of these rights are, see the Preface. Ironically enough, it is important that you reserve the same rights for yourself, with a few minor changes. As you read the Child's Bill of Rights, try restating each statement in an adult context.

When you do, you will see that this Bill of Rights applies to you, too.

Living your own life by rights doesn't just help you, it also helps you to parent your own children. Never forget that children model themselves after us whether we want them to or not. So behaving in a way that we want to see repeated is a good idea.

LEARNING
HOW TO PLAN

*a) In a healthy family there is organization; there is
    planning as well as the ability to respond to a crisis.*

*b) In an unhealthy family the members respond from one
crisis to the next, and when crises don't exist, create them.*

CHRIS SAYS, "Growing up in my family was like growing up in
a war zone. My father was a violent alcoholic and he'd come
home, bust up the furniture, and come after whoever was handy.
I learned to disappear pretty good unless my mom or sister was
around and then I'd take it so they wouldn't get it. I was in
combat in Vietnam, and while the other guys were shitting in
their pants, I felt right at home, crazy as it sounds. Actually, it
was better than home 'cause it wasn't chaos all the time and at
least I knew I'd eat regular. I stayed in the military because there
I didn't have to figure out what to do next. Just follow orders
and life works out, you know?"

If you grew up in a situation where you went from crisis to

crisis, it is not hard to understand why you would have trouble planning for the long term.

When you're a parent, knowing how to operate well in a crisis certainly comes in handy. Children are always breaking something, or dropping something, or falling, or whatever. Hospital emergency rooms are filled with parents and children of varying ages. Many accidents are preventable, but many are not. I have spent many hours getting my children stitched and x-rayed. I have often had fantasies of putting my children in a bubble of sorts to protect them from harm until they left home and I didn't have to watch. Dealing with crises is part of bringing up children.

I still remember an elementary school nurse who used to look down her nose at me as if to say it was my fault that my son had run backwards into a tree. I remember feeling intimidated and embarrassed and then foolish for feeling so intimidated and embarrassed and then feeling a little annoyed at my son that he was such a klutz, because it put me in a bad light. I confided my feelings to a close friend and her response was, "She does that to you, too? I thought it was just me!"

However, if everything becomes a crisis, life can begin to approach an obsessive-compulsive state. For example, many of the patients and students in my workshops on Adult Children of Alcoholics in the Workplace are ambulance drivers and surgeons and nurses in intensive care. The stress and pressure of these situations is not problematic to them; in fact, it is rather familiar to them. Like Chris, the vet whose story opens this chapter, crisis was all they knew growing up. It is fine to make these choices if they are made with awareness that there are options. But without this awareness, the choice is no longer a choice.

There are other advantages to being familiar with crisis aside from those that are apparent to parents, or those that make it possible to perform well in high-stress professions. Living in crisis teaches very valuable skills and an ability to be comfortable with certain styles of doing things. For example, a young adult with your history could make a decision to go out West for a vacation without needing to know anything except when she was leaving. This young person wouldn't need to concern herself with finding a hotel room or what she would do when she arrived in a particular city. This living on the edge would be part of the experience for her, as it might be for you. I've often said a COA could parachute out of a plane into a strange land with nothing but a backpack and without a doubt she would find her way.

These can be wonderful skills to have in certain life situations. But again, they are not always appropriate for all life situations. There can be a downside to living all of life "on the edge" or in a "winging it" state. In particular, it is not recommended that you choose this approach to life when you have three children under the age of five.

When you are traveling with small children, you need to plan ahead. You need to know there is an available and acceptable place to spend the night. Your children need to have more structure and order in their lives in order to feel safe and to be able to enjoy the experience of being children. Then, when they are adults, they can make a conscious choice as to whether to detail an itinerary or to wing it. Both options will be available to them.

Others of you who grew up in chaos probably find yourselves compulsively planning every second of every day, and every nickel and every dime. This too is a reliving of the childhood experience because this approach to things includes no space to test out a new idea or to change plans in the middle should something more interesting come up. This is also an unsettling environment in which to raise a child.

Either of these environments—one of no planning at all and one of compulsive and restrictive planning—will affect your child's ability to make career and other decisions in adult life. Since children learn by doing, either of these environments will affect your child's ability to make choices in a systematic way. They will either take the "just do it" approach and make a significant career or life decision just because it makes sense that afternoon, or they will so laboriously weigh the pros and cons of a particular opportunity or strategy that making a decision will become excruciatingly painful for them if they complete the decision-making process at all. So you also want to change the environment your family lives in to avoid recreating this for your children.

A sense of crisis on the one hand or systematic planning on the other is very often transmitted through attitudes toward school, behavior in school, and the ability to complete assignments. Your attitude will shape your child's ability to feel part of a functioning system and to complete tasks step by step.

A mother was anxious because her little girl was going to school for the first time. May's separation anxieties were as great as her child's, if not greater. Since May had no understanding of boundaries she was enmeshed with Samantha. Having her duaghter leave for part of the day was for May a loss of identity. For May, Samantha's rite of passage into her school years was a crisis.

May's situation is not unique. Many parents are anxious when their children leave home to go to school for the first time. I've often recommended that schools have get-togethers for parents who are experiencing this transition so they can welcome the experience and not pass along their fears to their children. The classroom is another sort of home for children, and all the home influences will be felt there, including a sense of crisis if that is what the parent imparts to the child. Some of the anxiety the adults feel will also have its source in the fear that others will find out what a failure they are as parents.

Separation anxieties exist for both parent and child. Once the child goes to school, both of them will have an adjustment to make. Neither of their worlds will ever be the same. It is important that the parents do their best not to convey their fears to the child. If the child picks up her mother's or father's anxiety, it will make the transition that much more difficult. If the anxiety is not addressed, a crisis can be created for both parent and child.

Once your child is in school, try to be aware of how your

own history impacted on you in the classroom so you do not pass your own expectations of crisis on to your children.

Many of you did very well in school. You got affirmed there. But even if you did well in school, the following principles may be useful to keep in mind as you raise your own children. Your children may not be the same as you. And you performed out of a system that you made up, not one that was worked out with and for you.

When you were a child you may have found yourself unable to concentrate during the school day because you were so filled with anxiety as a result of the stress at home. It is important for your children to try and have a relaxed atmosphere at home in the mornings before school. This is not always possible, but it is always possible to concentrate on starting the day in a pleasant atmosphere.

Many children dawdle in the morning. That can drive you up a wall. Expressing your frustration will not stop their dawdling, but it will ensure your morning ends up with crying or with everybody at everybody else's throat. Not the way to start the day.

You may have had to get yourself out to school or you may have been too fearful of your parents to dawdle in the morning and as a result you have no "good" memory to draw on to create a calm and systematic morning atmosphere. This can make things feel even more frustrating to you: "If I did it without prodding, why can't my kids?" But the truth is that your kids' lack of compliance is more typical than your compliance was. Although their dawdling is normal, you still need to get them out the door, but in a fashion as least chaotic as possible.

Some tips for a more relaxed morning atmosphere are:

1. Lay out clothes the night before.
2. Set the alarm a half hour earlier.
3. Make sure the kids take a vitamin supplement even if they refuse to down a full breakfast.

4. No doughnuts, Pop Tarts, or presweetened cereal. This will set your children up for mood swings, and the sugar they find on their own will be more than ample.

5. If your child should miss the bus and you end up driving him, don't use the driving time to berate him. Instead, ask the child if he has any ideas on how to keep this from happening again. Sometimes they absolutely do.

6. Don't add to the morning tensions. Your mood will determine the emotional keynote of your children's day.

Be prepared for the probability that a new baby in the house will generally cause a period of renewed morning dawdling. After all, your attention has been divided and it's not divided equally.

Bruce, the son of a client of mine, feigned illness one day soon after his new brother arrived because he thought he was missing out on something at home. I don't know what kind of spectacular day this kid thought his mom was having with the new baby during his absence, but his need to know made him curious enough to be too deathly ill to go to school. So Bruce's mom let him stay home but designed the most boring day she could for him.

The next day Bruce felt fine.

Bruce had reported a dream in which he found himself alone on the side of a river with everyone else splashing around and having a good time. Certainly his fears of having been pushed aside needed to be talked about and special time made for him, but there was no reason why it had to be made for him during the school day. The situation was not a crisis and did not require crisis intervention. It was something that could be dealt with within the context of the functioning family system. What was most important was that Bruce keep his routine and know his place in the family was secure even with a new baby in the house.

You may not have been able to develop good study habits when you were a child because of the chaotic atmosphere at home. It is hard to pass something along to your children that you yourself do not know. But good study habits teach patterns that will stand children in good stead in all aspects of their lives. The patterns they acquire by learning to study systematically are not skills that are no longer of use when they leave school. These are patterns that are good to have when they need to accomplish any project. Therefore:

1. Your child should do his homework the same time every day. Negotiate the time with the child. Some prefer to do it immediately after school and get it over with so they have the rest of the day free. Others prefer to do their homework right after supper. It doesn't matter what time kids do their homework as long as that time is consistent. Although I don't think television and homework are compatible, music seems to work for some kids, even if the music would not be your choice.
2. Homework needs to be done in the same place every night. So, a space needs to be found which is well lit and relatively uncluttered. The child can participate in the selection of the space. She does not have to be isolated unless it is her choice. Remember, homework is theoretically not punishment and should not be treated as such.

Helping your children with their homework is another Catch-22. I have always been available to help my children whenever they got stuck. They have all begged me to stop being so helpful. In math, particularly, while on their own a C or a B is possible, my help insures either a D or an F.

Occasionally I will be allowed to help with grammar, provided I don't assist with the text. Since I believe writing should communicate ideas and not necessarily be an exercise in intellectual gymnastics, I often need to bite my tongue. When I was shown an economics paper my youngest son was writing in which he referred to the "agrarian community," I couldn't restrain myself and asked, "Do you mean the farmers?" As soon as the words were out of my mouth, I knew I was in trouble. Once again I was not allowed to help.

This may be a generational failing in my family. When I was

in second grade I wrote an article for the school newspaper. My mother helped me with it. My teacher returned it to me and asked me to rewrite it. She said it was not up to my usual standard.

My mother said this had been the teacher's way of letting her know that she wanted me to do it on my own. She could tell I had done it with help because it was too polished for someone my age. I let my mother believe that, but to this day I'm not so sure.

All parents have at some point received a phone call from a teacher or been told at a parent conference that the child hasn't handed in his homework or is doing it carelessly. Chances are when your parents were told, you got yelled at or punished but your homework remained your problem. Chaos does not breed good homework. You, because you are now into perfect parenting without the tools, feel an overwhelming sense of guilt when your child isn't cutting the mustard. The teacher also has a way of saying without actually saying, "If you were any kind of decent parent your child would have perfect homework papers." Once again you feel as though you have been found out.

This is the point where you *must* put your own anxiety aside. You need to protect whatever self-respect you have left, but to set aside your anxiety in service to your child. You need to say to your child's teacher, "I would like to help my child and I need to know from you just exactly how you think this can be done." Write down what you were told because otherwise you'll forget it. Ask specific questions until it is clear in your mind what you can or cannot do to help.

If you came from a functional family you would not hesitate to get clarification of this type. You would assume you and your child's teacher were on the same side and you would not be seeking the teacher's approval. You would feel you had a right to get answers to your questions regardless of how fundamental they might appear to someone else.

But chances are when you were growing up, no matter what you did, it wasn't good enough. If you brought home A's, where were the A-plusses? If you brought home an A-plus the teacher was accused of being a fool. You were told to do many things without ever receiving full and complete instructions as to how to do them. As a result, you had no opportunity to perform your task correctly. And if by chance you were given instructions you could follow, the rules would change in the middle. Once again, there was no way you could measure up.

A man I know told me how his mother used to return the letters he wrote to her from college with his grammar corrected in red ink. Although he tells the story in an amusing way, it is not hard to sense how a part of him still winces at the thought. Needless to say, this man is not one to drop a note to keep in touch.

As a result of pressure of this type, many of you still struggle for perfection. Others of you simply give up altogether on trying to achieve certain tasks or goals. You have learned there is no intrinsic satisfaction to be found in doing well or doing your best or simply trying out something new to see how it goes. You have found there is no joy to be found in doing things systematically.

It is not unusual for teachers correcting their students' work to point out the mistakes without applauding what is correct. It is not unusual for a child of elementary-school age to bring home several pages of work with the number of questions answered wrong noted on top, without any sense given of the number right. In your growing up, what you did wrong is all that would have been noted. You could have done 195 out of 200 math problems correctly, but your parent would only have noticed the 5 errors. The message of how stupid or inadequate you were would come through loud and clear.

Turning this around so you do not pass this legacy on to your children is no small feat. You probably automatically want to criticize. It is the way you were taught to react. Criticism may be a motivator to do better, but even if you do better, even if you push to achieve in order to gain that elusive approval you hunger for, you will be unable to feel really good about your accomplishments. You will feel a relief that you were not found out. At least you have put off for a little while the inevitable discovery that you are a fraud and have accomplished good things only by accident.

Even if you are able to take in praise inspired by your achievement, your feelings of satisfaction and fulfillment will be elusive. You will be able to feel fulfilled in the moment, but you will not be able to hang on to those feelings, you will not be able to be truly nourished by those feelings, and you will have to continue to search for satisfaction.

Obviously you do not want your children to have the same experience in life. So your critical eye must be placed in check. Until your thinking changes, here are some guidelines.

First, if your child's teacher only marks the number wrong, take the time to figure out the number right. There is a big difference between "3X" and "97 C."

Ask if your child now understands how to do the incorrect parts correctly. Ask your child to take the time and show you. If your child still doesn't "get it," try and work it out with her. If you can't, encourage your child to ask the teacher for help. Place the emphasis on learning, not correcting.

We all have had the experience of wanting to say "What the hell is that?" when our child proudly brings home a piece of artwork. Next thing you know, the child is in tears because the masterpiece of the age has been sorely insulted.

It is better to say "Tell me about your drawing," or "What an interesting choice of colors." You may still get caught, but at least you tried.

The refrigerator is a great place to show off good schoolwork.

Bear in mind that not getting straight A's in grammar school does not mean your child will be drafted or can't go to Harvard. It also does not mean you have failed as a parent. What it may mean is your child does not have the maturity or motivation to do better. It also just may mean your child will not be a rocket scientist. Either way, it is not a sign that both you and your child are flawed.

Teachers love to put children in groups. Although you learned how to be compliant and to do as you were told, you never learned how to cooperate in a group. You probably either took over the group or did nothing at all to participate. Your children learn from you, so here again you need to teach what you never learned. It is not as hard as you think.

You can help your children to do this by encouraging them to participate in household activities. Setting the table or cutting the salad as someone else cooks teaches membership. In contrast, preparing the entire dinner on the one hand or not being involved at all on the other does not teach cooperation.

A cousin of mine once said, "Those who cook shouldn't have to clean up." This is an observation I took to heart. My cousin could just as easily have said, "Those who clean up shouldn't have to cook." Family members can take over specific tasks, or they can take turns doing them. The idea is that each family member does something but not everything. Yardwork can be done with the same flavor.

Developing a Responsibility Chart with the family is a good way to organize the chores. This chart will list who is to do what and when. Expectations are made known. Meet with the family and list all of the duties and responsibilities that must be handled. Everyone can choose which ones they will be responsible for and incorporate a system of rotation of duties and responsibilities.

A family discussion to plan an outing or solve a problem will also help in this regard. A ground rule has to be that nobody puts down anybody else's ideas. Everyone gets a chance to say what they think. A second ground rule is not to ask for opinions if your mind is already made up, since the decision is ultimately yours anyway.

The object of doing these things is to offer your child tips on how to be a "team player." The Responsibility Chart and the family discussion also develop a sense of belonging. This gives your child the tools with which to learn cooperation. If he doesn't do his part, if he is bossy or lazy or however else kids act, then at least you know you have done your part to teach a better way.

If you are called into school because your third-grader has an attitude problem, bear in mind that "all" eight-year-olds have attitude problems. Just because you were compliant when you were a child doesn't mean your child will be so, particularly if yours is a more normal household than the one you grew up in. The reality is that a child of eight can either concentrate on his schoolwork or sit still. I don't believe they can constitutionally do both at once.

As an elementary school guidance counselor, I was once asked to do a counseling group with ten young behavior problems. As a counseling group it didn't get too far. There was nothing wrong with these kids to begin with. Even so, the teachers were impressed with my work. The major benefit to them was that they got to have a break from those overly energetic youngsters.

Because of who you are, your children may be more street smart than their teachers. This poses an interesting dilemma. When this occurs you may have to align with the school because it is not always in the best interest of the child to be able to "outsmart" those in authority.

When one of my children was in all-day kindergarten, a well-meaning student teacher made an error which boggled my mind.

My child had apparently been very disruptive in the morning and then, once his energy was expended, had behaved appropriately in the afternoon. The teacher gave him a present as a reward for his good behavior. He was delighted with the present and with his discovery. For you see, he was the only child rewarded. The children who had behaved well all day were not rewarded. So he learned that in order to get a reward all you needed to do was improve. As a result, he had no incentive to change his ways.

I told him I was going to have a talk with his teacher, and any potential gains from this insight were history. Actually, what I said to my impish five-year-old was, "It worked this time, kiddo, but you won't be able to pull it off again."

I privately admit I thought the assessment was brilliant on his part, but certainly not one to be encouraged.

A second-grader was very disruptive in school one day. His

teacher said, "If you don't stop this behavior I'll keep you after school."

The child said, "You can't do that," and left.

In fact, the child was right. Legally, the teacher could not do that. The upset teacher called the child's parent.

In situations like these the parent must align himself with the school and tell the child, "You must do what your teacher says. You must work within the system."

Tehnically, the teacher doesn't have the legal right to keep the child after school and the child, being streetwise, knows this. However, it is not in the best interest of the child to be able to get away with knowing this. Codes of conduct are developed for the benefit of all concerned. Being able to do as you wish breeds chaos. Chaos does not help a child develop a pattern for living.

In school your children will be given both short- and long-term assignments. Your lack of experience with doing things systematically will, for example, make it difficult for you to help your children with a research paper since this has to be done step by step over several months. You will need to find out the details. Pick up a book on "How to Write a Research Paper," or "The Scientific Method," and don't allow your own fears of looking stupid prevent you from asking your child's teacher for the details of what, when, how, and even why to write a research paper. The teacher will perceive you as an involved and interested parent—not as a dummy.

Encouraging children to do their best in school shows interest in their development. Putting pressure on children for perfect performance may be serving your need and not your child's. Be sure to separate these two out.

The parent who brags that her child walked at nine months or was talking in complete sentences before she was a year is really saying, "My daughter walked at nine months. Aren't I wonderful?" It has very little to do with the child. Your child may be excited about gaining mastery over her environment, but trust me, at nine months old she may not be aware she is ahead of schedule. Actually, her sense of the situation will be more that she has just made the greatest discovery in the history of humanity.

The principles involved in doing things systematically are easily expressed, but will be hard to put into effect. It is very difficult to offer others a lifestyle that is different from your own. Operating under pressure may work for you and there is no need to change a pressured workplace environment. But in the home, a more relaxed atmosphere is preferable. If you start to feel you'll go out of your skin with boredom because there is so much consistency in the environment, then that is probably a sign you're doing something right.

Ironically enough, growing up in a more orderly environment will not be boring for your children. It will provide a structure both internal and external that will allow them to try out new things and work on new ideas without fear of loss of control.

SPECIAL
CONSIDERATIONS

ALTHOUGH DISCUSSED WITHIN the fuller context of this book, sibling, grandparent, "blended family," and single-parenting situations deserve treatment of their own. This is because these are situations that invariably add their own special brand of confusion to the mix.

SIBLINGS

Ginger came for counseling with a specific question: "My son and daughter, who are just about a year apart, are always fighting, and I feel like I spend half my life punishing my son. Is there a better way of handling this?"

It is usually a good idea to stay out of sibling spats if there is no danger that any bones or furniture will be broken. Spats will not last as long if you stay out of them. Sometimes I'll yell at my kids to cut it out, but rarely does it seem to matter who started it or who said what to whom. In general I have found all parties concerned to be equally obnoxious. My first question to Ginger took things in a slightly different direction:

"I'm curious about what it is your son is doing that causes you invariably to punish him."

"I'm not sure what it is," Ginger replied. "When I think about it, the only thing that makes sense is that I always felt so helpless as a child and so I guess I must identify with my daughter."

"Have you ever asked your daughter whether or not she feels helpless? She may not. And even if she does, there may be better ways for you to empower her than by punishing her brother."

"I hear you," she said, "and that makes sense to me. But now what am I supposed to do? I can keep my mouth shut or I can stop automatically punishing my son, but what do I do with these feelings? When I hear him picking on her, and I hate to admit this, I can't stand my own kid."

Next I asked Ginger what it was that set her kids off.

"Well, mostly my daughter complains that my son calls her names and teases her. And he complains that she takes his things without asking and then doesn't return them."

"Is that what happened with you and your brother?"

"No, my brother was much bigger than I was and he'd beat up on me when no one was looking, or he'd creep into my room when I asleep and put a dead spider on me. I still shudder when I think of it, and to this day I need a night-light. I would tell my mother what he did and she would accuse me of lying."

I pointed out that this didn't sound like the same thing at all.

"To be perfectly honest, I remember how powerless I felt when I was abused by my brother and how often I prayed someone would come along and take care of me and punish him for torturing me. It looks like I'm trying to fix my own history through my kids, doesn't it. And you're right. It's not the same thing."

Ginger's kids' normal sibling behavior acted as a trigger for their mother's sibling issues. Ginger's view of her own childhood was distorting her responses to her own children in the present.

When you deal with sibling issues, be sure you are responding to what is happening in the moment and that you are not flipping back into your own history.

As she gets clear about what she is really reacting to, Ginger's feelings will change. Next time her kids spat she will be able to remind herself that what went on in her life is not the same as what is going on with her children, and respond more appropriately to them. Ginger's children are typical, and fortunate that their mother is more available to them than Ginger's mother was to her.

If you grew up in a dysfunctional family, chances are your relationships were distorted as well. You may have had to take care of younger siblings and have experienced how they resented you for it. Or you may have acted out, and your siblings may have resented the fact that because of acting out you got more attention than they did. Or you may have withdrawn, and as a result not really connected with anybody in your family.

Over the last decade, the alcohol field has begun to help individuals suffering from alcoholism to get into treatment before their lives are totally devastated by their disease. This method is called "intervention." Family members and others significant to the patient's circle confront the patient with how his behavior is impacting on them. The preparation for this encounter involves people discussing the past and how they felt about it. During this process, many brothers and sisters share their feelings about their childhood for the very first time: "I didn't know you felt that way. I thought it was just me. I'm so sorry. Had I known, I could have been there for you."

Up until that discussion takes place, many brothers and sisters have never shared feelings with each other. They discover that in effect they have grown up side by side alone together.

If this description sounds as though it fits your relationship with your siblings, this past history will set you up for much confusion in terms of what is an appropriate sibling relationship for your kids in the present. For example, as a result of your history you may have developed the fantasy that if you are a good parent, your children will get along and be agreeable companions. You may be of the opinion that if yours is a functional household, there will be no fighting and no bickering.

Forget it. Prepare for another fantasy to bite the dust. Sibling rivalry is alive and well. Siblings, just because of the simple fact that they are siblings, always have a love/hate relationship.

If your family is one in which caring feelings are shared, experiences are shared, and one in which the members are really there for each other, then this model of interaction will become available to your children. That is the good news.

The bad news is that if your family is more open than your parents' family was and as a result your children are more open than you and your siblings were, all the feelings you learned to repress as a child will be right out there, right up front.

And when feelings are not repressed you get the whole panorama. You not only get the feelings you want to see, but you also get the angry ones. It's good to be more open, but it's also more volatile. And if you start talking about your feelings in the way that's been suggested in this book, anger is one of the feelings that is probably going to come up.

A good example of a situation in which this will happen is the arrival of a new baby. The baby will be a delight to all but will also bring up feelings of jealousy. As far as your other child or children are concerned, your attention has been diverted elsewhere. This jealousy can be eased if the older children can participate in the baby's care, but remember that you have not failed as a parent if your kids tell you to send the baby back.

You can also count on your children to compete with each other for your approval and attention and to accuse you of playing favorites. For instance: "Why won't you let me if you let her? Why can't I have it if you gave it to her? You like her better. You don't love me . . . ," ad infinitum. When you raise children in a functional family, the kids fight and bicker.

I know a family where the kids can yell and scream at each other or sometimes even fight. But let anyone else even do so much as say something unpleasant about one of these siblings, and that kid will find they have to deal not only with the kid who has been slighted or hurt, but also with that kid's brothers and sisters.

This is a healthy sibling relationship, and parents should

expect similar patterns in their kids. It's not easy to live with, but don't be fooled into thinking that healthy is easy to live with. A repressed child is much easier to live with than a normal one any day of the week.

There are other benefits to not raising a repressed child, although for parents who have to live with the process the blessing may sometimes appear to be mixed. For instance, when Isabel started her freshman year in college and a lot of the other kids were going out and getting drunk, she chose not to. She reported to her mother, "There was no point. I'd already done that."

Isabel's parents had a mixed reaction to this development. On the one hand, they were pleased she had the maturity not to act out in this way. On the other hand, they were a little envious of those parents who hadn't had to live through this particular stage of their child's development. It's not preferable for this to happen at all, but it does. And a child expressing herself while she's growing up at home doesn't act like someone being let out of a cage for the first time when she leaves home for school.

It seems to me it may be time to develop support groups for parents.

Soon after Nina's new baby arrived, Nina's husband, Cal, was called out of town on business. The business responsibility was one Cal had to assume, but it left Nina alone with both the new baby, Andrew, and her two-year-old, Eric. Money was tight, and Nina could not afford many sitters. Her family lived far away, and to top it all off, Nina and Cal had recently relocated to the area, so she did not yet know many mothers with kids the same age.

All of this added up to frustration for Eric. Suddenly, after spending all of his time alone with his mother, this toddler was spending every minute with his mother and the new baby, who had very time-consuming demands. Instead of playing and making noise with his mom the way toddlers do, Eric was supposed to be very quiet so the baby could sleep. Instead of sitting on his Mom's lap, the baby sat on Mom's lap. Instead of going out to play, Eric had to stay inside with Mom and Andrew.

Soon Nina was on the phone to me, wondering why it was that every time she turned away her two-year-old seemed to be beating up on the baby. Hard. And a couple of times, Nina had seen no recourse but to hit Eric to stop him. She knew this was not the right approach and was beside herself with guilt and confusion about what to do.

After we talked for a little while, it became clear that Eric missed spending time alone with his mother and that this what was making him so angry. It also became clear that Nina, who had grown up in a more repressed home, was not without her overreactions to Eric's behavior. I suggested a few networking methods, and Nina soon found a few other mothers who took turns keeping each other's kids for a few hours at a time. Nina and Eric got to spend more time alone in ways that were appropriate for a toddler, and the sibling rivalry has begun to approach a less extreme level. Nina now feels less desperate and more in control.

Networking is absolutely essential when you're a parent. It's essential because you have to get a break, and it's absolutely essential when you have more than one child, so you can spend independent time with each of them. If you can't afford a sitter or your partner is unavailable for whatever reason, it is important that you and your friends learn how to network. The truth is that two sleeping babies are no more work than one sleeping baby is. And in certain circumstances, watching two toddlers can be easier than watching one, because the toddlers can entertain each other.

If you don't know mothers with kids who are the same age as your kids, try asking your pediatrician for the names of other mothers who do and who live near you. And remember that sometimes your childless friend would adore spending a little time with the baby. You might want to try attending a parenting seminar or support group. And playgroups for kids the same age are forming all the time.

It may be small comfort, but remember that what is going on in your home is probably going on in most other homes that have children your kids' age. It's all very trying, but it is also normal. That's the part that may be new to you, so be careful not to overreact. Your kids are not out to drive you crazy—not on purpose, anyway.

GRANDPARENTS

Katherine sat down in my office and began to sob.

"I watch my parents with my children and it makes me churn inside. I would have given anything for them to have treated me the way they treat Benny and Margie, when I was a kid."

Grandparents play a special role in the lives of their grandchildren. That role is a simple one. It is to adore them and to spoil them rotten. Typically, grandchildren can do no wrong in the eyes of their grandparents, and after spending time with grandparents it can take a while to get children back into their normal routine.

This can be a problem for you as a parent, but it is wonderful for the children and the grandparents. If your grandparents fulfilled that role in your life, you know what I mean.

If your parents were not affectionate to you but are now doting grandparents to your kids, don't be surprised if you find yourself feeling jealous of your children. If your parents are more attentive to your children than they were to you, it is hard not to feel this jealousy. The situation brings your own unresolved feelings of deprivation to the fore. Bear in mind that you do not feel jealous because you want your children to be deprived the way you were, but rather because their relationship with your parents makes you feel your own loss more acutely.

You may still be enraged at your parents for the way they treated you, but don't withhold your children from them to get even with them. It's not fair to your children, and their welfare is primary. You may argue that your parents are no different than they ever were and that they'll undermine your kids just like they undermined you. But this is not necessarily so. Remember that your influence on your kids is much stronger than your parents', and your parents' views may have little effect on them.

My mother was a real neatnik who needed to have everything "just so." As far as she was concerned, the only good child was a clean child. I, on the other hand, raised my kids believing that kids get dirty and they need to be allowed to get dirty. When my kids went to visit my mother, I'd be afraid they'd come back thinking I was inadequate because my mother would say things to them such as, "Does your mother allow you to go out like this?" When my kids spent time with my mother, it was true that they did have their faces washed more often and that they did clean their plates and that they never had a shoelace untied. But she adored them and they adored her and they realized the neatness was her problem and not theirs. And contrary to my fear, they did not get confused trying to figure out how to say the right thing to protect their mother. As they grew older they wore their hair longer whether she disapproved or I disapproved. But they were rebelling against me and what I represented, and not against her.

Maribel, a young Hispanic woman who grew up in this country, was very concerned about the way her in-laws, who had grown up in Central America, treated her four-year-old son Alejandro. Mari said that Alex still wanted a bottle when he took his nap. But when he was spending time with his grandparents, the baby felt compelled to hide while he took the bottle because his grandparents didn't believe it was "manly" to drink from a bottle. In addition, while Mari enouraged Alex to cry if he was upset, her in-laws had a "macho" attitude that men didn't cry. All of this made Maribel feel very defensive and confused.

This is an interesting dilemma because the issue is a cultural one. The grandparents love their grandson and are very warm and giving to him. Their attitude toward Alex is not a punitive one. He is not adversely affected by their attitudes. The greatest consequence of their behavior seemed to be the worry and concern it instilled in the baby's mother. The grandparents were not saying these things to be punitive, but merely because that was the way men were supposed to behave in their culture.

The reality is that Alejandro will live in both cultures—that of his parents, and that of his grandparents. So this is not a battle worth fighting. Instead, Mari can teach Alex "In our house we do things one way, and in Grandma and Grandpa's house they do things another way. When you are with them, it might be a good idea to go along with them."

This advice applies to any child living in two cultures. This way the child has choices and does not have to be confused or embarrassed.

However, this advice assumes a visit with grandparents once or twice a month. If the grandparents have regular babysitting responsibilities and you have concerns like these, you may have to develop clear ground rules as to whose rules get followed because they may conflict and your guidelines need to be the firm ones. In this situation, you need to think carefully about which things really matter to you and about which other things you cannot give way on. You will also need to let go of those things that are not essential. This will be difficult for you to do since you are such a black-and-white thinker. Do it anyway.

If you were physically and/or sexually abused by your parents, *do not* decide your children are safe with them. *Do not* decide your parents would never lay a hand on your children.

If the family secrets about the abuse have been exposed and you have made it very clear that what happened was damaging to you and to the entire family system and that you are committed to making sure abuse never occurs again, and if both the perpetrator and also those who stood silently by admit to their responsibility for the abuse and go into treatment to extinguish this behavior, and if you and their therapist both feel confident the therapy has been successful, *then and only then* may you decide to be less guarded about letting your kids be with your parents.

If you believe my recommendation is excessive, you are still in denial on some level.

If these conditions have not been met, then you are putting your children at risk. Unfortunately, the reason I know this to be true is because of my clinical experience, which has shown me the results of not meeting them. Sick people behave in sick ways and your wishing it were different will not make it so. Doing this is like asking a drunk to behave sober. It just doesn't happen. To the undiscerning eye it can sometimes look as though a person is no longer sick or no longer behaves in sick ways, but this appearance is merely for show.

If one of the ways you managed the stress of being a victim was to shut down feelings, you may still be doing that. And although the predictable feeling one has about leaving a child with a known abuser is panic, this feeling may not be available to you because of your history. Because of your history you may feel nothing at all, and since you either need the help with your child or don't want to deal with the unpleasantness you are certain will result from disappointing your parents, you will tend to rationalize your decision: "They're older now." "They've changed." "They adore their grandchildren." "They won't be harmed."

Doing this will put your children at risk.

A friend of mine had been used sexually by her father while she was growing up, as had been her sisters. Greta had been in therapy for several years trying to overcome the effects, which included dealing with her conviction that her mother had been aware of what was going on but had not intervened.

One day Greta called me in a rage. Her niece Beverly had dropped by to see her as she often did, and while they were chatting Bev had said, "I hate it when Grandpa puts his hands all over me. When you hug me it feels great, but what he does feels funny. I told my mother, but she says he's an old man and I'm just being silly. Do you think I'm silly?"

"No, I don't," Greta had replied. "No one should touch you in ways that feel funny. It doesn't matter *who* they are."

Next Greta confronted her sister. When she did, Hannah turned pale and left the room.

Greta then decided her father had gotten away with this behavior for long enough.

"I may not have been able to take care of myself," Greta told me on the phone, "but I sure as hell wasn't going to let Bev become a victim. When I confronted my father and told him what a slimy bastard I thought he was and what I would do if he ever laid another hand on a child, he was calm as ice. 'Still the troublemaker,' he told me. 'Some people never change.'

" 'Your f—— ass, I'm a troublemaker, and don't you ever forget it,' I replied. So he didn't deny it. He just turned the tables on me the way he had done for my whole life. But I didn't care. Bev was free, and strangely enough, so was I.

"And oh yeah, P.S., my mom just said nothing and left the room, just like always."

"Your sister Hannah behaved like your mother," I said, "and would have sacrificed her daughter as she had been sacrificed, in order not to face things. How fortunate that Bev had you."

If you don't know how to handle letting your parents know you will not allow your children to be alone with them, or if the thought of doing so makes you very anxious, see a professional and come to grips with this. There are no acceptable but . . . but . . . buts. None at all.

You are the parent and you are in charge. You are not there to take care of your parents except where appropriate. This applies not only to abusive situations, but also to the caretaking situations in which many parents with children find themselves at some point or another, and in which others have spent many years.

Carla complains, "My whole life was spent taking care of my mother. There was always something wrong with her. I grew to resent her bitterly even though I still take care of her. She went from one illness to another. And I'm not certain that all of them were real. However, it was my job to take her to the doctor, to

give her a bath, to do her shopping and whatever else needed to
be done. I still do it even though I have a family of my own.
And I am good for nothing else. If I don't, the guilt is so overwhelming.

"Now that I am getting older I am all the more conflicted.
How can I turn my back on her now? To tell you the truth—
and I hate to admit this—I'm looking forward to the day
she dies. It's not fair to my own kids because I'm not there for
them. They resent me, and I don't blame them. But I feel so
powerless."

The parent who demands enmeshment makes the process of
individuating extremely difficult. Many spend their lives in this
struggle only to have to face it again when their parents are old.
An enmeshed parent is one who is overly involved with her
children and who demands her children be overly involved with
her. This is a situation in which the boundaries have been
blurred.

Becoming separate from such a parent means having minimal
and controlled contact with that parent. It is very difficult to
overcome the enmeshment and have your autonomy without
keeping careful watch over the relationship. When the parent's
need becomes greater, which can occur with age and illness,
contact between parent and child usually becomes more frequent
and once again the struggle becomes more exaggerated, the way
it was before individuation took place. This is nobody's fault.
It's just one of those things that happens, because the tie between
parent and child is so strong. Still, your first responsibility is to
your own children.

If you are in this situation, one thing that will make sense is
for you to learn what community services are available for your
parents and how to allow them to access these services so you
don't have to do it all yourself. Sometimes your doing some of
the groundwork will save everybody a lot of time, energy, and
aggravation later. There are home-care services and food services.
There are senior citizens' groups, and often there is special trans-

portation for senior citizens. For specifics, try calling the American Association of Retired Persons (AARP) or check your parents' local phone book.

You are the generation in the middle and you will feel an obligation at both ends. It is important to be clear about what level of responsibility is appropriate and what level has more to do with having spent a lifetime caretaking. Your primary responsibility is to your own children. Their needs must come first. Make decisions about accommodating your parents only once these needs have been met.

It was Father's Day but Lisa really didn't want to visit her father. She just wanted to spend the day at home with her family. Lisa looked at herself in the mirror and asked, "Will I be able to live with the guilt if I don't go? After all, how many more Father's Days does he have coming?"

Lisa's answer to herself was no, she was not prepared to live with the guilt. So she and her family loaded up the car and made the trip. Lisa's father died suddenly a few months later, and although his death would not have been her fault if she hadn't gone, she certainly would have been haunted by the "if onlys" if she had not chosen to make that particular visit.

Other members of the generation in the middle make other choices. Jim's mother called him up out of the blue one Sunday to let him know she was expecting Jim and his whole family for dinner in a couple of hours. She had gone out and bought the food and cooked it and then called Jim up and made her announcement.

Jim's plans for the evening had been to stay home and relax. As difficult as it was for him, Jim had to tell his mother, "I would love to come, but we need more notice."

The only way to effect a change in behavior is to change the given response to a given behavior. Changing the response has to change the behavior. In the future, Jim's mother will no doubt give Jim more notice if she wants to invite him and his family over, or be less surprised when Jim says no. And Jim will feel good about having the courage to take care of himself by defending his boundaries.

If he can do this without becoming angry with his mother, it also sets a good example for his kids. His kids will know how to set boundaries of their own without getting angry about it: "I feel so bad that we cannot come. Please give me more notice in the future."

And then there are the creative solutions. Marvin had not been to visit his mother for eight years even though she lived in a nursing home he passed every day on his way to and from work.

In our session, Marvin explained why:

"I simply can't deal with what happens to me when I see her. I hate not seeing her but I'm at a loss as to what to do."

I asked Marvin if there was any amount of time he could spend with his mother that he could enjoy without feeling diminished. Marvin replied that his limit was no more than five or ten minutes. I pointed out that a five- or ten-minute visit to an elderly person might be very good for them, and that his mother might not even be looking for more. Marvin went.

These are hard choices but they *are* choices.

The Blended Family

A friend of mine who was recently divorced reports the following comment made by his twelve-year-old daughter: "Daddy, I don't know if you will find someone and remarry or not, but I can promise you that if you do, I will hate her for the rest of my life."

There you have it. The idea of the ideal blended family is just one more powerful fantasy that most of us enter into when we choose new partners. Even the idea of having a "blended" biological family is a mythical one. Just because people share the same biological parents doesn't mean they "blend" with each other. Frankly, I only use the term "blended family" because it's in current usage and not because it makes any sense.

Kids try to hang on to the notion that somehow, some way, their parents will get back together. Any new person who comes onto the scene is a potential threat to that fantasy.

In addition, children feel the loss of the noncustodial parent and are fearful that the "new person" on the scene may take their other parent away, too, and then they'll be left with nobody.

And if you both have kids, these feelings are going to persist on both sides.

So there you are. The two of you have high hopes not only to have your relationship work out better than last time, but also that this time you will be able to offer a warm, supportive, loving, communicative home life for the children.

The pitfall: What happens when you offer this terrific environment to the children? How do they respond? Do they respond, as you hope, with just as much love and support as you feel?

Not on your life.

The response is generally hostile. If the children find themselves responding to what you offer, they will feel disloyal. Rather than live with that uncomfortable feeling of disloyalty, they will become hostile. And the harder you try, the more hostile the children will become as they yearn for what you have to offer.

I once asked the stepdaughter of a friend of mine about her feelings for her mother and stepmother. Lynn's stepmother was the one who initiated the contact between me and Lynn. Gaby was very confused and upset: "Every time Lynn and I begin to get close and spend some good time together shopping or having dinner, the next thing I know she backs away and we have no connection for weeks."

When I discussed this with Lynn she said, "Yeah. That's right. I get all ripped up inside and I don't know why."

I asked Lynn if she would be willing to show both relationships, the one she had with her mother and the one she had with Gaby, in a drawing. Just draw circles to represent yourself and your mother, and yourself and your stepmother.

MOM   LYNN   STEPMOM   LYNN

The drawings clarified matters. Although Lynn and her mom get along, Lynn doesn't feel really connected to her mother. Lynn obviously feels more connected to her stepmom, but backs away from this closeness. Lynn is afraid of the intimacy she shares with Gaby, never having known it with her own mother, and these feelings also make Lynn feel disloyal to her mother. She ends up conflicted and deals with her inner conflict as she has dealt with conflict all her life—by running away and avoiding the issue, which is something else Lynn and I discovered in our time together.

But this conflict was one that wasn't going to go away. It had to be addressed. Both Lynn and Gaby needed to understand the emotional mechanism at work, because otherwise they would think that the relationship and the good times they spent weren't good for either of them. Bringing all the issues out into the open by talking about the drawings took the pressure off the child. She got to express her feelings to her stepmother, and those feelings were in turn validated by Gaby. The relationship prospered.

Try making these drawings yourself at home if you have this problem. It works for any kid of any age who is able to understand the instructions. And it's not below the interest level of teenagers, either.

Another example of good intentions not working out as hoped involves the eight-year-old boy of an abusive and neglectful father. Gray, the new father, was attentive, warm, loving, and willing to drive in the car pools and go to the soccer games and do all the other things that caring fathers do.

Meanwhile, Will, the child, became nasty, spiteful, ungrateful, and unmanageable. When times were stressful, Will had always been compliant and congenial. Yet now within this greatly improved family situation, he had become impossible.

Therapy showed that Will was overwhelmed by his feelings. Gray's kindness had made him acutely aware of how unkind his biological father had been to him. The result was that the child became enraged. If Will acted out against his natural father he would lose him entirely and would have to give up hope that his natural father would ever be there for him. As a result, Gray "got it" instead. After all, Will had had things under control until Gray came along.

A third example involves children who believe that with their parents' divorce, they have finally won the oedipal battle. The child has finally got her parent all to herself. And what happens, *someone else* comes and starts taking a share of the parent's affection, time, and attention. Feeling displaced, the child competes openly for the attention of the desired parent. In situations like these, the best thing to do is make it clear to the child in question that he or she is still cared about. Sometimes children need to be taught that love comes in great supply. The more we love, the more we *can* love. So a parent's loving someone new does not mean loss of love for the child. Attention may be diverted sometimes, but as children develop, more of their attention will be diverted, too.

When new siblings come to the blended family, other issues and feelings come to the fore. On one level, there is some enthusiasm on the part of the kids for having new brothers and sisters. But at the same time there is also competition and a fear that the original parent will love the new kids more. This fear is particularly pronounced concerning the parent the kids don't live with if the stepbrothers and sisters do.

Then there are the seemingly endless variables that are always at play in these newly complex family situations.

Bob reports, "During the early years of our relationship Millie and I used to refer to the crowded couch. Mil and I would sit on the loveseat in the living room to try and sort out a problem, and whenever we did, it would become very clear that the little couch where we were sitting was actually very crowded. There were the ghosts of Millie's kids, my kids, her ex, my ex, her parents and relatives, and my parents and relatives. All on the same two-seater couch. True, not all of these characters would be involved all of the time in every situation we had to work out, but particularly when the kids were concerned, few discussions were uncomplicated."

All is not lost. I do not present this to depress you or to make you flee. But you do have to know what is real, and folks who grow up in troubled families get caught up in what they want to be true and in believing that if they just try hard enough they can make what they *want* to be true *be* true. What they lose sight of is the power that other people may have in keeping things from working out the way they hope things will, no matter how hard they themselves try.

There are many things folks in a blended family can do to make things more functional. In particular, there are some principles that couples can follow to improve the situation:

1. Make a commitment to communicate with your partner on a daily basis. Make a commitment that you will hear each other out and both be honest with your reactions and your feelings. Agree that you will not be afraid to disagree, but that you will also be open to another point of view.

2. Recognize that you feel differently toward your stepchildren than you do toward your own. This may mean you favor your own kids or it may mean you bend over so far backward to not play favorites that you neglect your own. It's a tricky balance.

3. Very often the stepparent can see the stepchild's behavior more realistically than the biological parent can, and can offer useful suggestions to the biological parent that he or she would otherwise be blind to. It may also be that you are automatically defensive whenever there is a criticism. You may feel your

inadequacy as a parent has been uncovered and you may want to cover it back up again.

4. Sometimes a stepparent can offer support when the child is in a difficult spot with the biological parent. This doesn't mean you can take sides, but it does mean you may be able to help them both get unstuck. For instance: "Yes, you're right, your son has no right to be that disrespectful. By the way, did you know he just got cut from the team?"

5. Be sure the family boundaries are clear-cut. This makes family members feel more secure. Ideally, family rules should be clear and consistent. They should also make sense to those they govern. To whatever degree individuals believe that what is required of them is fair, that is the degree to which they will go along with the rules without resistance. (Boundaries are discussed in another chapter.) You will have to support the boundaries and limits your partner sets regardless of whether or not you agree with them. If you disagree, share it at a later time without children present. Otherwise the children will manipulate both of you and all the relationships involved will deteriorate as a result.

Keep in mind that coming from a troubled family yourself, all of these issues and problems and your responses to them will be exaggerated. What this means is that you may have to take careful thought before you take action. Which may mean removing yourself from the situation until you do that. What it doesn't mean is that you take no action. Sometimes, because of your history, you'll be more tolerant than is appropriate.

I remember saying to a woman not too long ago, "You're allowing his children to abuse you just the way your parents abused you. You need to tell them in no uncertain terms that such behavior is unacceptable in your house."

This woman was flabbergasted by my observation. She hadn't realized she was being abused and she didn't know she had rights, too. Because you may have extreme or confused reactions, when it comes to your blended family you want to make especially sure you go by the guidelines set down in this book.

In summary, sometimes you have to put yourself in difficult situations in order to get something else you want out of life. So if the person you choose to spend your life with comes into the relationship with children, that is something you will have to adjust to.

After all, the two of you are on the same side. And ultimately the difficulties you face as a unit will strengthen your relationship and will benefit the children as well.

SINGLE PARENTING

Darnelle called me, close to hysteria. "I can't do it any more. It's too much for me. That son of a bitch just walks away and I have to deal with the whole damn mess of it. I've had it. Enough! I'm screaming at the kids, I'm making mistakes at work, I have no social life . . . I just don't know what to do."

Darnelle was suffering from a case of single-parent burnout. It does happen, but it's not inevitable. There are ways to relieve the pressure so it doesn't get to the stage Darnelle is at. Clearly Darnelle needs some relief and direction.

Research shows that at least 50% of all children will spend some time in a situation where there is a single parent, so this is certainly a subject that deserves careful attention.

It is my belief that "going it alone" is far superior to living and bringing up children in a hostile environment.

It also doesn't have to be so terrible. I say this because there is a prevailing belief that being a single parent is a terrible state to be in and that if one is in it, one needs to be very sorry for oneself.

Firstly, give up the notion that you are now both mother and father to your children. That is simply neither possible nor desirable. Although we live in an age where we encourage androgyny and women develop their male sides and enter the workplace fighting for equal pay and equal rights and men are encouraged to develop their female side and demonstrate feelings and tenderness, men and women are still not the same. Men and women often have a different worldview, and although both can offer safety to a child, the way they offer this safety may be expressed differently.

Unless you are widowed or have adopted children as a single parent, your children's noncustodial parent may want to continue in a parent role. Many noncustodial parents become more interested in their children once they don't see them every day than they ever did when they shared the same physical space. Many do not. Some abdicate entirely and others just entertain their children and are not available emotionally even though they consider themselves loving parents.

If you are divorced you may be very angry. It is tempting to use the children as a way to settle scores and even to deny access. Your children need to be able to connect with both parents, however, and even though you can influence them now, unless being with their noncustodial parent puts them at risk from a condition such as active alcoholism, denying them time with their parent is not in their best interest. Although punishing your ex-spouse may feel satisfying to you, you are taking your needs and not the needs of the children into account when you do this.

Frankly, doing this is not in your best interest either. You need some time away from the children for your own mental health. They will not love their other parent more because that parent buys them things or is not the one who sets down limits for them. They will not love their other parent more even if they use this type of love as a threat when they are angry at you: "Daddy never screams at me. I wish I lived with him."

Daddy can be calm because the time he and the kids spend together is limited and child-focused. There is no need for the two of you to compete. If the noncustodial parent stays involved, everyone benefits.

Whether or not your kids' noncustodial parent remains involved in their lives, they still need the benefit of both a male and female point of view.

A single parent who is female needs to network with men who can provide the direction and/or point of view that only a man can provide, particularly with male children.

For example, when my sons would get into fights in the normal course of growing up, my stomach would tie up in knots and I would be afraid that my "babies" would be hurt. It didn't matter who started the fight, what precipitated the fight, or that my sons were perfectly capable of taking care of themselves. I knew enough to keep some of these thoughts to myself, but I would consult with male friends of mine. Their response was, "A guy's gotta do what a guy's gotta do." Clearly, they did not share my panic.

I also never thought it was my role particularly to discuss my sons' reaching puberty with them. I thought man-to-man would be better.

A young man I know whose parents had divorced asked his mother if he could see a counselor.

"Of course," she said. "But can't I help?"

"I don't think so," he responded. "You're part of the problem."

When the boy saw the stricken look on his mother's face, he simply said, "I have to talk to someone about the idea that you might be with a man other than my father and how I feel about that."

He was absolutely right. That was an adjustment he would have to make, but it was not for her to be the one to help him through that process.

The same is true of the single parent who is male and the child who is female. You can't be the one who tells her what it feels like to menstruate or to help her pick out her first bra or to take her to the gynecologist. Chances are she may have other areas of "girl talk" that she would like to discuss with a female adult which you would not greet with enthusiasm.

Again, one of the keys to successful single parenting is know-ing how to network. You are not the only one in your position. There are many others, and if you are isolated you will become overwhelmed. There are simply not enough hours in the day to manage all alone. If you're looking for a new home, check to see how many swing sets are in neighboring yards or how many strollers are in the hallway. Knock on the door and see who is a single parent. Groups and seminars also exist for single parents. There are other methods, too. See the "Siblings" section of this chapter for some more suggestions.

You probably have to work, which means your children are either in school or day care, so you have to:

1. Get them up in the morning and ready to go as well as get yourself up and ready to go;
2. Get them to school and yourself to work;
3. Pick them up;
4. Worry about the grocery shopping, the cleaners, etc.;
5. Fix dinner;
6. Make sure homework gets done;
7. Make sure baths get taken;
8. Get them ready for bed;
9. And oh yeah, "quality time." You are always available to listen and listen, always involved, always warm.

When do you get to relax with a hot tub, a cold drink, and a trashy novel?

When do you get to go to lunch with the girls?

When do you attempt to date?

When do you buy yourself a new outfit?

After the kids are in bed, chances are you simply collapse and pray you will get your clothes off before you pass out.

When I was a single parent with kids at home, I remember visiting my internist because I simply couldn't breathe. He checked me out, found nothing physically wrong, and started to laugh. Of course, I saw nothing funny about the situation.

Finally he said, "Well, I'd think in your line of work you'd have this one figured out already. Where is your breathing space?"

He was right. I had none. Along with my usual responsibilities, my children were needy and needed Mom's ear. And Mom's ear was always ready. I had reached a place where I simply had no room to breathe.

All my priorities were in order except one. Me. Somehow that had to enter the mix as well.

It is not hard for things to get out of balance, particularly if you are a caretaker by nature. It's an easy trap to fall into, but does not present an ideal role model for your children. Martyrs are rarely, if ever, appreciated in their lifetime.

If you need time alone, say to the children, "If you're not bleeding, don't knock on the bathroom door when I'm taking my bath." Your time alone doesn't have to be dramatic. It just has to be private.

Which brings us to the subject of the next chapter.

T H I R T E E N

TAKING CARE OF
YOURSELF

PARENTING IS A big job if done conscientiously. There will be periods of extreme joy and times of unbelievable frustration. There will be moments of great pride and of great embarrassment.

The child you care for will give you much pleasure and will love you back. You will also watch the child you nourish develop under your care and you will be able to take pride in that growth. The parental role you assumed as a child was a thankless job that earned you no reward. It earned you nothing but abuse and emptiness. You had all of the work and none of the joy of parenting. But this time around, you can find that just being in the presence of your children can make you feel warm inside and help give meaning to your life.

This doesn't mean there will always be perfect harmony in your home and it doesn't mean your children don't ever have to pay attention to your feelings. It simply means your loving care will be responded to in kind.

Another person worthy of your loving care is you yourself.

Taking care of yourself is good for your children and good for you.

One of the most powerful ways of teaching your children the type of adult you want them to become is to be who you would want them to be. Essentially, the idea is to behave in ways you would want your children to imitate. Consider these:

1. *Don't neglect your nutrition.* Not only children need to eat what is good for them. As you get older you will not have the iron stomach you had as a kid, and you will pay a health price if you ignore this fact. You should eat regular meals, not just grab things on the run. Cook for yourself when you cook for your child. You may not think you can do both of these at the same time, but you can. Balance your diet. If you need to, read books about nutrition and follow their advice. You'll also probably have more energy to deal with your life if you eat well. (Don't worry—certainly some of your current basic principles will continue to apply, including the ones that say stale cake has no calories and neither does food eaten while shopping.)

2. *Exercise regularly.* When your children are little, running after them may be aerobic enough, but as they get a bit older, you may have to develop a formal regime. Walking is great. Exercise is not only good for your body, it also helps to reduce stress and alleviate frustration. I know a woman who insists her children take that mile walk with her every day. It works out well for all of them. They get to spend time together and the exercise works out some of the kids' endless energy, so they all end up more relaxed.

3. *Address your spiritual side.* Regardless of whether or not organized religion works for you, it is in your interest to accept the idea that there is a power greater than yourself. Going to church may or may not be the answer. Reading books, meditating, learning yoga, or appreciating the sunset may tap into this aspect of life for you. It is also my belief that every time the children leave the house and our watchful eye, we give up control to a higher power. Somehow, in order to let them go, we must believe they will return safely. The risk to their life and limb as they explore their world does not diminish as they get older. If only they could be wholly protected until they go out on their

own. The acceptance of a higher power and the ability to give over their care to it can offer a measure of serenity.

4. *Maintain a sense of humor.* If you lose your sense of humor, you have lost, period. A friend of mine left her three-year-old son and his buddy to play in a "childproof" room in her home while she and the other mother relaxed with a cup of tea. After about ten minutes of uninterrupted bliss the mothers went in to peek at the kids. Somehow, some talcum powder had been left in this "childproof" room. The little darlings had managed to manipulate the top and completely powder the entire room and themselves. My friend said to me, "I looked at that white mess that was my son and knew I had three choices. One, I could kill him. Two, I could drop to my knees and bawl my eyes out. Three, I could laugh at this totally ridiculous sight. Somehow laughing took the edge off and through the miracles of a vacuum cleaner, holding my breath, and a bathtub, things got under control."

5. *Don't slight significant others.* Although your children are a primary relationship they are not your only relationship. If you have a spouse or lover, that relationship does not automatically always have to take a back seat to the kids. Children will take you over twenty-four hours a day every day and it is up to you to set the boundaries. If they come between you and others in your life in an unrealistic way, you are doing them and yourself a disservice. You need to have a balance in your life and your children need to know what their place is in it. This will also give them a role model for their own future.

A child may complain about being left with a sitter, but if the sitter is trustworthy and caring and if the child is not continuously being shunted off and feeling neglected, or going through a fearful stage, the complaint can be duly noted and the child can be left for the day or evening anyway. More often than not, the complaining ends once the door is closed and the tyrant is no longer in control.

One of the most frustrating things about parenting is the isolation. It is important to spend time with peers and without the children. If there is no sitter available to you, you and your spouse may have to take turns going out or you will go stir-crazy.

6. *Keep your mind alive.* This may involve reading or joining a study group or taking a class. Otherwise you will find your mind is totally absorbed with diapers and car pools and little else. You need to set boundaries with your kids, i.e., "You're reading and I'm reading. Sometimes I'll read to you and sometimes you'll read to yourself." You may have to reinforce this many times. It will work eventually, G-d willing.

7. *If you work outside the home, do whatever you can to minimize the housework when you are home.* Some people prepare several meals at one time. Some people throw comforters on the bed rather than dealing with bedspreads. Anyone who is still ironing children's clothes needs to (1) have her head examined, and (2) buy no-iron clothes instead. If you don't have a dishwasher there is no law against using paper plates, maybe not all of the time but certainly some of the time.

In addition, find ways for the children to share tasks with you. The children need to be with you. What they do when they are with you is secondary to this contact. So-called "quality time," which is supposed to be when you are glued to your kid and vice versa, is difficult to come by, and the end of the day is nobody's quality time. So make any time you have to spend with your kid quality time. Any time you have to spend with your kid can be a sharing time. It can be a loving time. *Real* quality time is time that can be spent sharing life, and those hours are unfortunately very limited.

8. *Choose your children's caretakers carefully.* Interview, check references, and test someone out before hiring her or him on a regular basis. The need to rely on caretakers may become more and more a function of the lifestyle of our era, which means that more and more often someone other than you will be present to take care of the boo-boo or adjudicate the fight. Since the other caretakers in your children's life will be strong influences on them, be sure they are people who share your values. That will help you ease your mind when you are away from the children.

It has often been said that you cannot truly love another unless you can love yourself. I'm not certain I agree. But I do know that the place to begin is to treat yourself in the same loving ways you treat others. This chapter has pointed the way toward some of them, and as you try them out you will certainly find more of your own.

LOOKING BACK AND
LOOKING FORWARD

YOU MAY HAVE used this book to help you decide whether or not you want to have children. Or it may have answered some of the doubts you had about yourself if you had children before you were ready.

What to do now?

That is the subject of this chapter.

A woman I met on a ferry said to me, "I feel such great sadness about what I did to my children. When I was young the only strokes I ever got were for my looks, so I spent all my time being sure I looked good. I had nothing else. I was empty inside and had nothing to give. I had no skills. I was so disorganized that I couldn't even help my kids with school projects. By the time I found the scissors I'd be too frazzled to go any further. I had no right to have children, but I didn't even know that.

"Now that I have worked long and hard on myself, I am much better equipped than I was, and I can be more loving. I can love them now and certainly be a better grandparent than I ever was a parent. I just hope it's not too late."

The time to have a child is when you feel ready for it.

You may have to take care of yourself first. There is nothing wrong with that. As a matter of fact it can be a very good idea.

You may have been a parentified child and feel that it is your turn now: enough of being there for everybody else. *What about me?!*

These feelings are certainly understandable. You may be sick to death of giving and getting nothing in return. You may have had it with taking care of the needs of others. You were a parent as a child and it felt lousy. You may want to experience the childhood you always wanted even if you are a grown-up. There is nothing wrong with that except if you are or are thinking of becoming a parent.

You cannot have it both ways. You can play with your children, but parenting is not child's play. If you decide to become responsible for young life, once again you get to give and give. You get to take care and you do not get to be taken care of.

That's the way it needs to be. If the thought of that turns you off, then being a parent is not for you. And there is nothing wrong with you if you have these feelings. Having them is only problematic if you already have children.

If you are at a stage in your life where it is important to you to get your own needs met and not be constantly giving and are ambivalent about having children, then it makes sense to wait. You need not judge yourself for feeling this way. Just be clear and don't decide that you want to be a parent only because others are putting pressure on you and you believe you "should." Remember that these "others" will not be living with the outcome day and night, night and day.

You may have already had children and been, for whatever reason, unable to provide a healthy environment for them. Your awareness of your past behavior and your wish that it could have been different may leave you feeling guilty and helpless. Although the past is the past and you can't do anything about that, changes you make now in the present can influence your future. This is true for you and it certainly true for your children, regardless of their age.

At a lecture that I gave recently at Rutgers Summer School for Alcohol Studies, a man in obvious distress raised his hand and asked, "Is there any way that I can rectify the mistakes in my past? As part of my twelve-step work I made amends to my children. I felt a little better, but it didn't change anything for them. Is there any hope?"

If you already have children, some of you may be asking yourselves similar questions.

Here are the answers. If your children are still small, you absolutely have a chance to turn things around. If you find you cannot practice the principles found in this book on your own, seek out a family counselor. This process will be very new to you, and very different because it is so new.

If your children are grown up, you need to make a different kind of amends. The amends you make in twelve-step programs have to do with telling those you have harmed that you regret your past actions. This is an important part of your journey to recovery because it helps to unload some of the guilt of your past actions and attitudes. The amends you must now make to your children in this regard involve inviting them to tell how it was for them and *listening* to how they felt about what went on, what happened to them as a result of it, how they feel about it now, how they feel about you now, and what they think you can do to help them heal. Only after you have heard them out and they are satisfied they have said what is in their minds and hearts, and that may take a long time, can you tell them how sorry you are and how sick you were at the time. Your reasons, excuses, and rationalizations come last, if at all.

This process will be excruciatingly painful for you, and the guilt you feel will be enormous. Be sure and have a support system to help you through the pain of it.

If you go through the process you will feel better because you will have done all you can do. Reading this book will teach you how to break those patterns in the present that were so damaging to you and your family in the past.

Keep in mind that underneath all the pain and anger, your children love you the way you love your parents. Keeping the pain and anger bottled up inside keeps a lid on the love and protects them from future hurt. If they let go of the bad feelings, the love too can be released and the healing can begin for all of you.

CLOSING

You may not feel just informed at this point, but also a little overwhelmed with how much there is to learn about parenting and how much is involved in parenting.

It is certainly understandable why you have these feelings, but there is also a bright side. Much of parenting is a natural instinct. Most species have a natural instinct for taking care of the needs of their young and keeping them out of harm's way, and ours is one of them. The natural world also insures that those creatures who are a threat to the welfare of the young of any particular species are more unusual than usual. So since you are already so concerned with being a good parent, chances are you will have what it takes to parent well.

Although parenting is new to you, you do not have to reinvent the wheel to be successful. When you feel insecure, bear in mind that others before you have also felt insecure and others before you have come up with ways that work.

I remember the day a friend visited my house with her first baby and struggled to find a way to put the baby on the sofa so he would not fall off onto the floor. It was an insurmountable task.

Since I had been through this myself I asked, "Would you mind if I made a suggestion?"

"Not at all," she replied.

"Why not put the baby on a blanket on the floor? That way you don't have to worry about him falling off something."

It's much simpler to be a good parent when you know how to take advice. Unsolicited advice can be a real nuisance and undermine what little self-confidence you have, but if you choose your advisors carefully, there are many out there who can be valuable resources to you.

This book has provided you with tips on how to avoid pitfalls in parenting. Always bear in mind that the compliance of children is not the measure of good parenting. A knowledge of right and wrong and the ability to make responsible choices are much better measures. Even knowing this you will make mistakes. It is important that you make mistakes. If your children see that you are not always perfect but will apologize when wrong and make amends, then they will be freer in their own lives and will learn how to apologize or make amends for their own mistakes.

Compliance makes for peace, and no one questions the desirability of that. But enjoying the energy of children will encourage cooperation and joy.

And as you gain a sense of how much is involved and worry about whether you are up to it, don't lose sight of the fact that those perfect people with those perfect children who were toilet-trained at birth, play the piano by ear, never get dirty, get straight A's, are captain of the football team, never talk back, are king and queen of the prom, get full scholarships to the best schools, and never gain weight, get pimples, or break a leg are just plain *boring*.

I remember that one day I was walking down the street

with my three children when my daughter suddenly said out loud, "Look, there's that look that Mom gets on her face when she's with her kids and she's not angry at *any* of us."

So lighten up. Be a kid with your kid. Have a good time, get mud in your shoes, and who knows—you might even find out that parenting can be *fun*.